AUDIO ACCESS INCLUDED

FIRST 50 RIFFS & PATTERNS

YOU SHOULD PLAY ON RHYTHM GUITAR

One-of-a-kind collection of must-know rhythm parts
for blues, rock, jazz, and country styles.

by Dave Rubin

To access audio, visit:
www.halleonard.com/mylibrary

Enter Code
1809-1175-7510-7310

ISBN 979-8-3501-2716-4

Visit Hal Leonard Online at
www.halleonard.com

World headquarters, contact:
Hal Leonard
7777 West Bluemound Road
Milwaukee, WI 53213
Email: info@halleonard.com

In Europe, contact:
Hal Leonard Europe Limited
Dettingen Way
Bury St Edmunds, Suffolk, IP33 3YB
Email: info@halleonardeurope.com

In Australia, contact:
Hal Leonard Australia Pty. Ltd.
4 Lentara Court
Cheltenham, Victoria, 3192 Australia
Email: info@halleonard.com.au

CONTENTS

Blues

4 Example 1: Open-String Cut-Boogie Pattern
5 Example 2: Barre-Chord Cut-Boogie Pattern
5 Example 3: Dominant Seventh Barre Chords
6 Example 4: Dominant Ninth Chords
6 Example 5: Dominant Seventh Inversions
7 Example 6: First-Inversion Ninth Chords
7 Example 7: Dominant Triple Stops 1
8 Example 8: Dominant Triple Stops 2
8 Example 9: Basic Boogie Woogie Pattern 1
9 Example 10: Basic Boogie Woogie Pattern 2
9 Example 11: Postwar Electric Blues
10 Example 12: Postwar Chicago Blues 1
10 Example 13: Postwar Chicago Blues 2
11 Example 14: Postwar Texas Blues

Rock

12 Example 15: 5ths and 3rds
12 Example 16: Power Chords
13 Example 17: Power Ballad with Common Tones
13 Example 18: Flamenco Music Derivation
14 Example 19: Moving Bass Line
14 Example 20: Bo Diddley Beat
15 Example 21: Major Triads
15 Example 22: Chord Melody
16 Example 23: 50s Rock 'N' Roll 1
16 Example 24: 50s Rock 'N' Roll 2
17 Example 25: 50s Rock 'N' Roll 3
17 Example 26: 50s Rock 'N' Roll 4
18 Example 27: 60s Rock
18 Example 28: 60s Boogie Rock
19 Example 29: 70s Boogie Rock 1
19 Example 30: 70s Boogie Rock 2

Jazz

20 Example 31: Swing Era 1
20 Example 32: Swing Era 2
21 Example 33: Swing to Postwar
21 Example 34: Jazz Rock
22 Example 35: Prewar Jazz 1
22 Example 36: Prewar Jazz 2
23 Example 37: Prewar Jazz and Beyond
23 Example 38: Jazz Arpeggios 1
24 Example 39: Jazz Arpeggios 2
24 Example 40: Jazz Arpeggios 3

Country

25 Example 41: Bluegrass 1
25 Example 42: Bluegrass 2
26 Example 43: Postwar Nashville 1
26 Example 44: Postwar Nashville 2
27 Example 45: Postwar Nashville 3
27 Example 46: Country Rock 1
28 Example 47: Country Rock 2
28 Example 48: Country Rock 3
29 Example 49: Modern Nashville 1
29 Example 50: Modern Nashville 2

BLUES

EXAMPLE 1: OPEN-STRING CUT-BOOGIE PATTERN

Classic Example: "Almost Grown" (Chuck Berry)

Based on boogie woogie piano, this riff is perhaps the most identifiable blues rhythm of all time and can be found in countless rock 'n' roll standards. It perfectly suits a 12-bar blues in A, laying easily on the fingerboard due to the open strings 5 (A), 4 (D), and 6 (E) matching the I, IV, and V chords, respectively.

EXAMPLE 2: BARRE-CHORD CUT-BOOGIE PATTERN

Classic Example: "Bright Lights, Big City" (Jimmy Reed)

Open-string riffs and chord progressions are limited to a finite number of keys. However, if you play them as moveable fretted patterns (as with barre chords), you can access virtually all keys. In this example, use your pinky for the last two notes on strings 6 (A7) and 5 (D7 and E7). A similar riff using the signature move from the minor 3rd to major 3rd can be heard over the V–IV turnaround in "Bright Lights, Big City."

NOTE: For this example, and the remaining blues riffs and patterns, one measure of the I, IV, and V chords are notated. In each case, you can expand the example into the full 12-bar blues form.

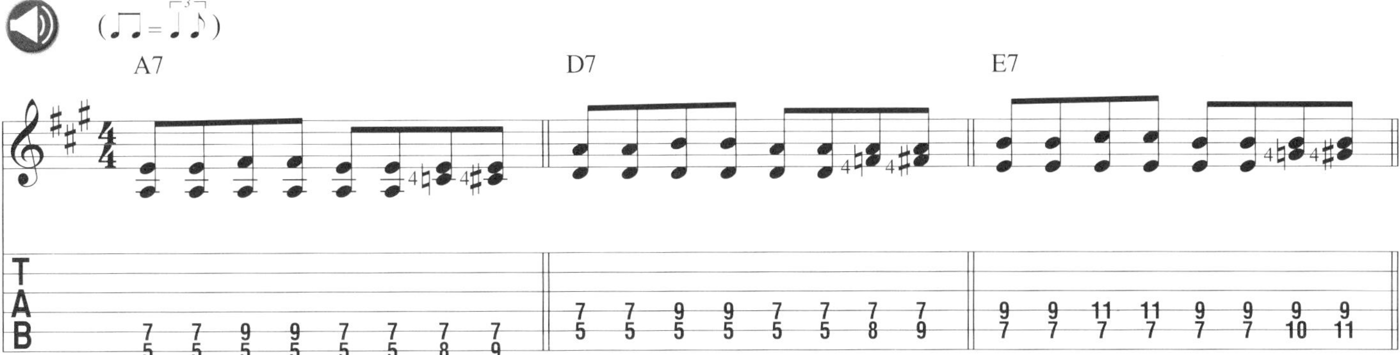

EXAMPLE 3: DOMINANT SEVENTH BARRE CHORDS

Classic Example: "Time Is on My Side" (The Rolling Stones, Brian Jones on rhythm guitar)

These basic chord forms are found in many different types of music and work well as an alternative to the 12-bar "Cut-Boogie Pattern" found in Example 1. While presented here as four strums per measure in 4/4, there are many different ways to strum and divide the measures. In 12/8 for example, you could create a triplet feel by playing four groups of three, accenting the first strum of each grouping: **1** 2 3, **4** 5 6, **7** 8 9, **10** 11 12. To get the most out of this book, experiment with different strumming patterns and rhythms for Figures 3–8.

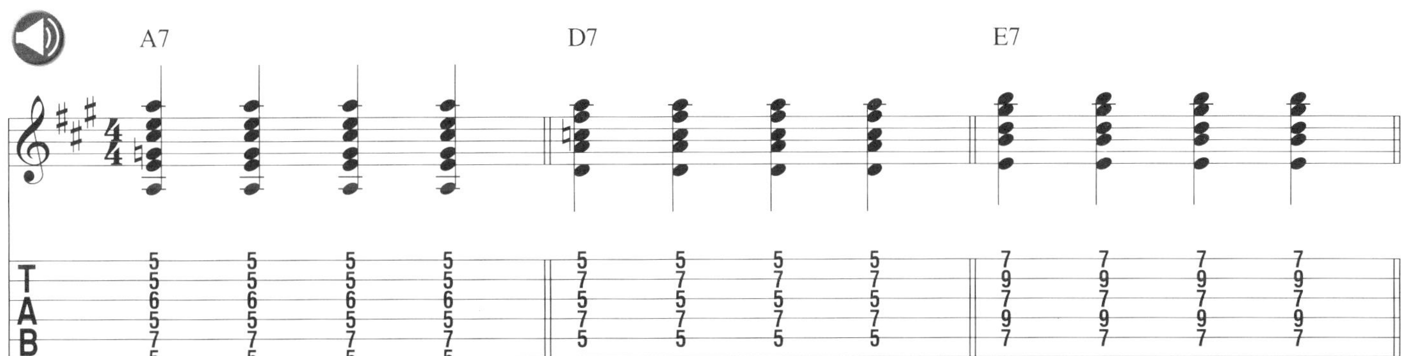

EXAMPLE 4: DOMINANT NINTH CHORDS

Classic Example: "Stormy Monday Blues" (T-Bone Walker, as performed by Bobby "Blue" Bland)

A more advanced alternative to Example 3, this example uses *dominant ninth chords*. We can build dominant ninth chords by taking each dominant seventh chord from Example 3 and adding a ninth to it—adding B to the A7, E to the D7, and F♯ to the E7. The moveable D9 (IV) and E9 (V) voicings from this blues pattern are also regularly found in jazz and funk music.

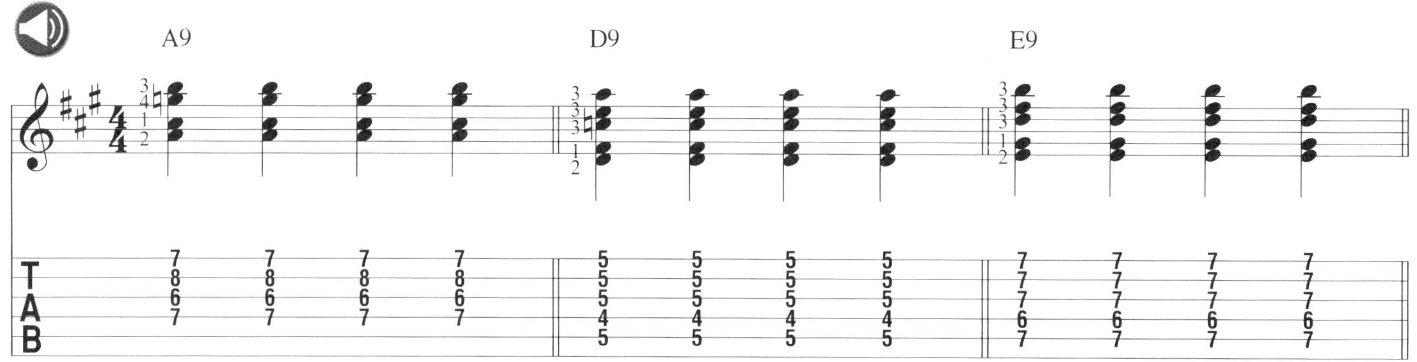

EXAMPLE 5: DOMINANT SEVENTH INVERSIONS

Classic Example: "In the Open" (Freddie King)

A chord is said to be *inverted* when it's not in root position—i.e., when a note other than the root appears in the bass. For example, A7 contains the root (A), 3rd (C♯), 5th (E), and ♭7th (G). In *root position*, the root (A) is in the bass. In *first inversion*, the 3rd (C♯) is in the bass, in *second inversion* the 5th (E), and in *third inversion*, the ♭7th (G). For our chord progression below, A7 remains in root position, but D7 and E7 appear in second inversion. In the music, inversions are noted as chord symbols with a slash, such as D7/A (read "D7 over A").

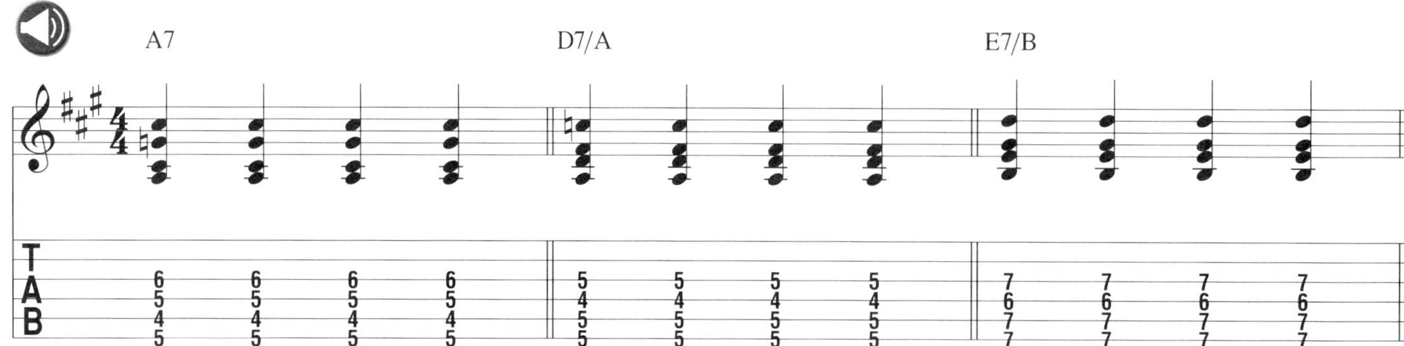

EXAMPLE 6: FIRST-INVERSION NINTH CHORDS

Classic Example: "Call it Stormy Monday" (T-Bone Walker w/ Jazz at the Philharmonic, Live in UK 1966)

The chords in this example are *rootless voicings*—i.e., chords that don't contain the root. Looking at the first chord A9/C♯, we can see it is in first inversion (the 3rd in the bass). Furthermore, without the root A present, the notes C♯-E-G-B form a minor 7 flat 5 chord (C♯m7♭5). This idea—using a m7♭5 chord starting on the 3rd of a ninth chord—is a common rootless voicing to use in jazz, blues, and funk. For the final two chords, our original ninth chord voicing is used (from Example 4), albeit with the bass note removed. To hear the implied harmony of this progression, you'll need a bassist or other instrumentalist to lay down the root notes.

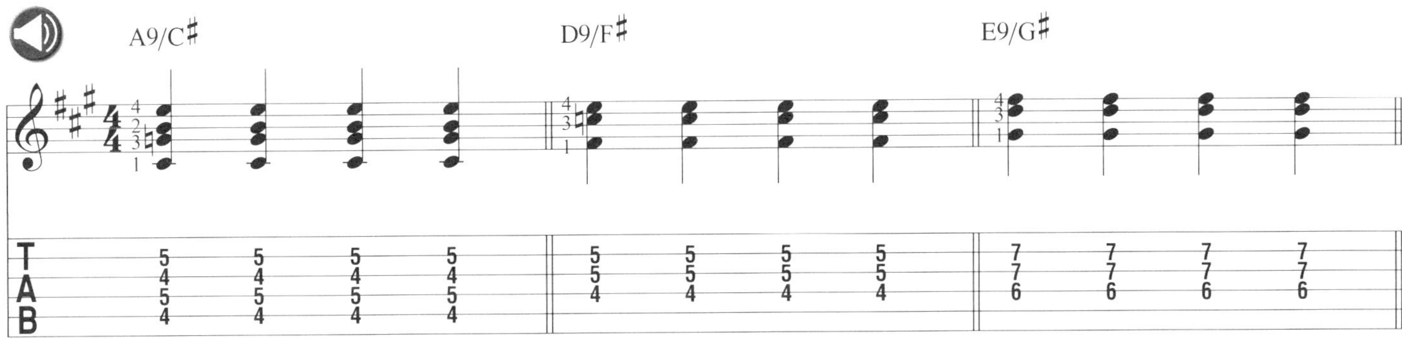

EXAMPLE 7: DOMINANT TRIPLE STOPS 1

Classic Example: "Fast Boogie" (Little Walter)

A *triple stop* is a chord containing three notes. Like Example 6, we'll use a rootless voicing for A7, but in this case, it's in second inversion. Triple stops for D7 and E7, played on the top three strings, follow. Reminiscent of a horn section, voicings played on the top three strings can add an upper register edge to an accompaniment. They can also be used to complement other rhythm guitars or keyboards playing in the middle or lower registers.

EXAMPLE 8: DOMINANT TRIPLE STOPS 2

Classic Example: "Night Train" (Jimmy Smith and Wes Montgomery)

This example uses the I chord (A7/G) in third inversion (♭7th on the bottom), while the IV (D7/F♯) and V (E7/G♯) chords are in first inversion (3rd on the bottom). They are fatter sounding and (arguably) "cooler" than the trebly triple stops from Example 7. In addition, the combined I and IV chords include the notes G, C, and E from the A blues scale, making scale embellishments more accessible when desired.

As in Example 6, these voicings do not contain the root note. Hence, they are most effective when fleshed out with a chordal accompaniment in root position by another musician or a bassist playing the roots.

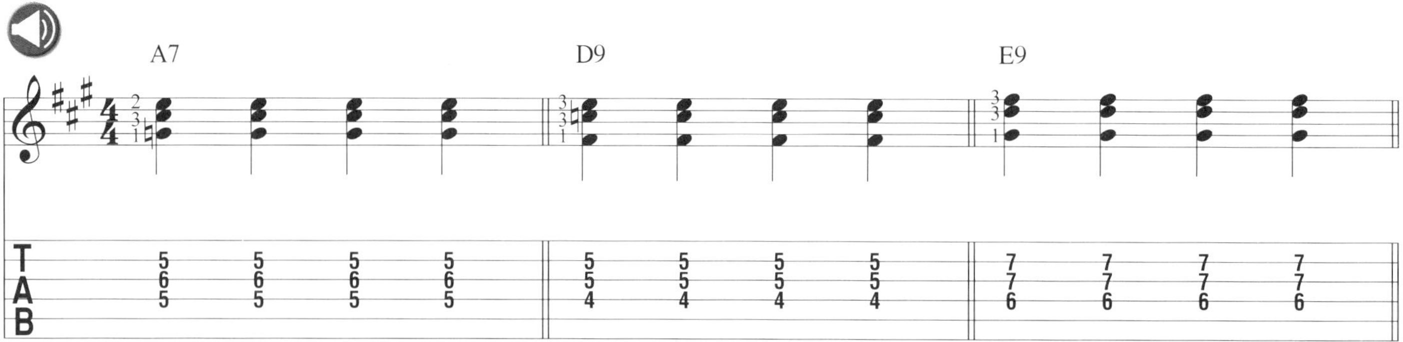

EXAMPLE 9: BASIC BOOGIE WOOGIE PATTERN 1

Classic Example: "Linda Lu" (Ray Sharpe)

Returning to riffs, Example 9 is fully fretted, so we can move it to any key by starting the pattern on the roots of the I, IV, and V chords. While it is generally recommended, and considered good technique, to play alternating down and up pick strokes when playing eighth notes, this pattern packs more punch with all down strokes and a staccato feel (play the notes short and clipped).

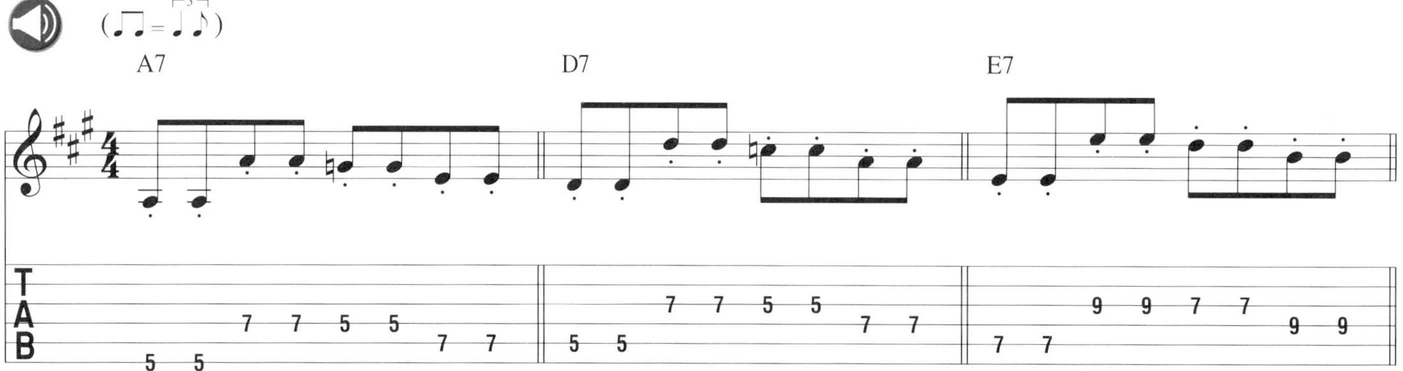

EXAMPLE 10: BASIC BOOGIE WOOGIE PATTERN 2

Classic Example: "What'd I Say" (Ray Charles)

Example 10 is a variation on the boogie woogie pattern from Example 9. It's often heard in faster tempo songs, such as Ray Charles' "What'd I Say."

EXAMPLE 11: POSTWAR ELECTRIC BLUES

Classic Example: "Stormy Monday" (T-Bone Walker, as performed by The Allman Brothers Band)

Just as triple stops contain three notes, *double stops*—commonly called dyads—contain two. Play the dyads in this example with your second and third fingers fretting the notes, aspiring to emulate the sound of a horn section with legato glissando. In addition, while we are only playing dyads, we are creating tension by starting out implying a major 6th chord before the stepwise resolution to the 5th of the dominant seventh chord. To hear this, play the open fifth, fourth, and sixth strings for the A, D, and E, respectively, on the first beat of each measure.

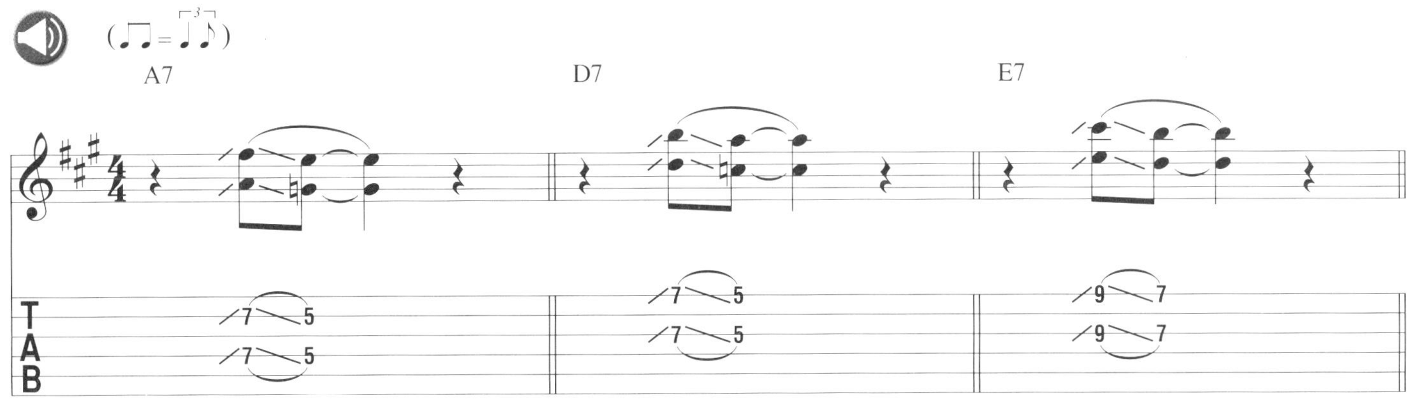

EXAMPLE 12: POSTWAR CHICAGO BLUES 1

Classic Example: "Keep Loving Me Baby" (Magic Sam)

This example is the most basic form of the postwar Chicago blues pattern and is an effective way to embellish I–IV–V chord changes. For the I chord, barre the second and third strings at the seventh fret with your third finger. Follow with a first-finger barre at the fifth fret and a concurrent hammer-on with your second finger to the major 3rd (C♯) on the sixth fret. For the IV (D9) and V (E9) changes, utilize third- and first-finger barres for the same-fret dyads. A common variation features a trill between the fifth and sixth frets of the third string over the I (A) chord.

EXAMPLE 13: POSTWAR CHICAGO BLUES 2

Classic Example: "Shake Your Money Maker" (Elmore James)

The second example of postwar Chicago blues features a dyad riff based on 3rds. Like Example 12, when both notes of the dyad are on the same fret, use a partial barre with the first finger covering both the second and third strings. When the dyad spans two frets, use your first finger for the lower fret on the second string and your second finger for the higher fret on the third string.

EXAMPLE 14: POSTWAR TEXAS BLUES

Classic Example: "San-Ho-Zay" (Freddie King)

For this postwar Texas blues example, we'll be using syncopated strumming. First, think of each beat being broken up into eighth notes—**1** & **2** & **3** & **4** &. If we assign downstrokes to the downbeats and upstrokes to every upbeat (the "&" in between the beats), we get: down-up, down-up, down-up, down-up. Follow this strategy throughout the riff, pairing downstrokes with downbeats and upstrokes with upbeats. Observe how the syncopation adds "swing" to the rhythm.

ROCK

EXAMPLE 15: 5THS AND 3RDS

Classic Example: "Locomotive Breath" (Jethro Tull)

Double stops in 5ths—colloquially known as "power chords"—are one of the prime building blocks of rock rhythm guitar. In Example 15, the A5 utilizes the open fifth string, so only your first finger is needed for the note on fret 2. For E5 and G5, use your first and third fingers. Note that the C chord is a dyad built on a major 3rd interval (not a power chord), which can be played with the first finger on the second fret, fourth string, and the second finger on the third fret, fifth string.

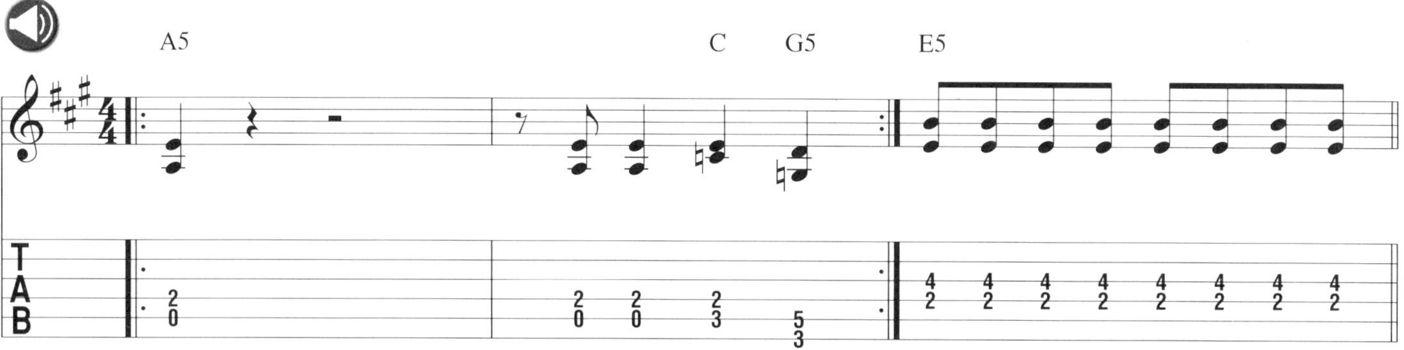

EXAMPLE 16: POWER CHORDS

Classic Example: "Train Kept A-Rollin'" (The Yardbirds)

A variation on the straight power chord, Example 16 uses open bass strings to add interest and momentum. We are in the key of E minor here, moving between the ♭III and IV chords, but with the 3rds dropped, the major/minor tonality of each chord is blurred. When soloing over this progression, the E minor pentatonic is the scale of choice.

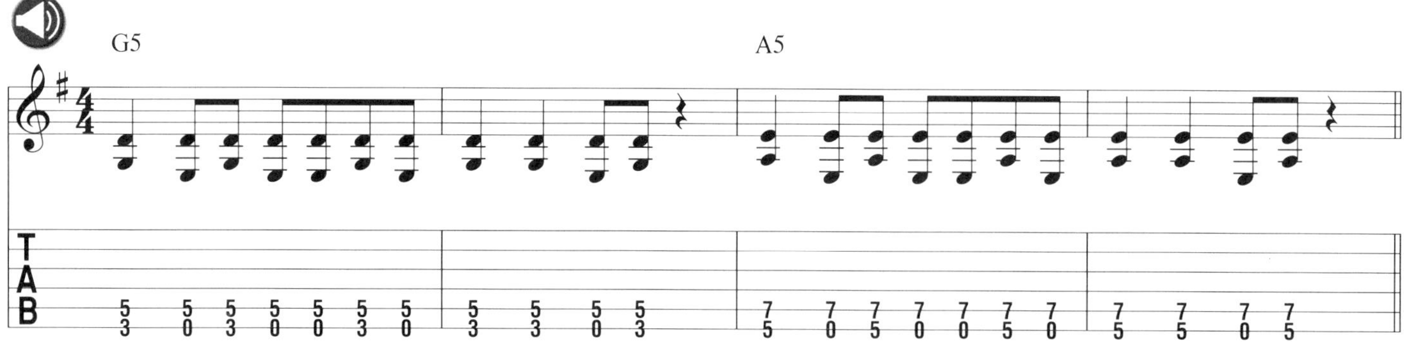

EXAMPLE 17: POWER BALLAD WITH COMMON TONES

Classic Example: "Stairway to Heaven" (Led Zeppelin)

Chord progressions with common tones provide smooth connections between each chord while maintaining harmonic variety. Observe how the progression builds subtle forward motion as the G, C, and Dsus4 chords ascend in pitch. The common tone G links the first three chords, before the D major V chord resolves the tension of the Dsus4. In addition, the D creates a strong pull back to the I chord G. While "Stairway to Heaven" doesn't use this exact I-IV-V progression, the technique of common tones to connect chords is abundant.

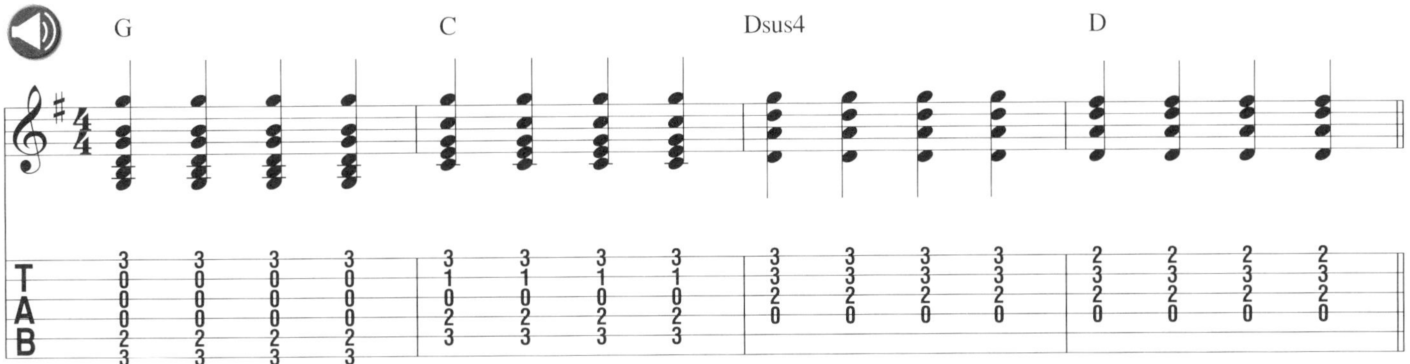

EXAMPLE 18: FLAMENCO MUSIC DERIVATION

Classic Example: "Babe, I'm Gonna Leave You" (Led Zeppelin)

Derived from flamenco music, the power of this dramatic descending progression has not been lost on rock musicians. Some well-known songs containing variations on the pattern are "Walk, Don't Run," "All Along the Watchtower," "Turn to Stone," "(Don't Fear) The Reaper," "Carry on Wayward Son," and "Sultans of Swing." While it's common to play the progression with barre chords, this example uses an open Am chord and descending bass line to form Am-Am7/G-F♯m7♭5-Fmaj7. Use your fourth finger for the low G of Am7/G and your thumb over the top of the fretboard for the F♯ and F of F♯m7♭5 and Fmaj7, respectively.

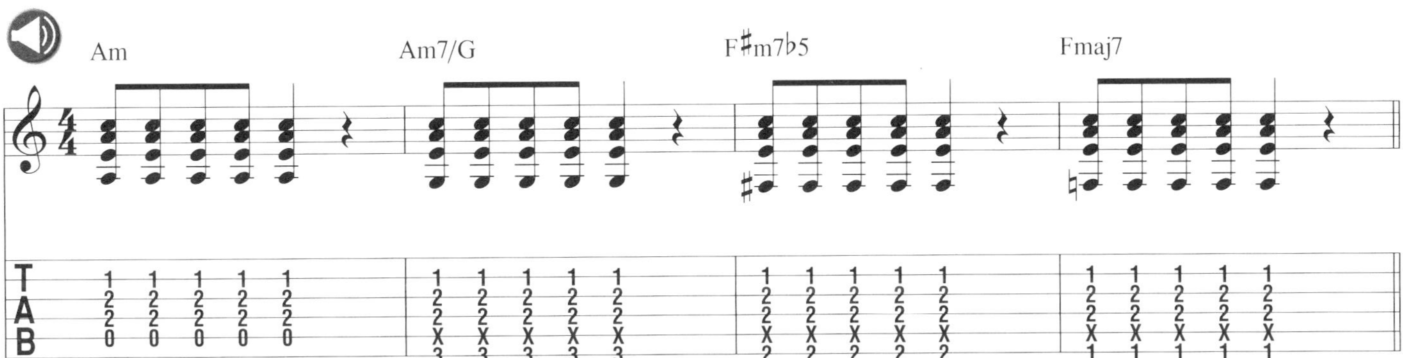

EXAMPLE 19: MOVING BASS LINE

Classic Example: "The Weight" (The Band)

To execute this progression, you will need to barre the A chord throughout with your first finger, avoiding the first string with the pick. Utilize the third finger for A/G♯ and the thumb over the top of the fretboard for A/F♯. Notice how the descending bass line of A–G♯–F♯–E is derived from the A major scale.

EXAMPLE 20: BO DIDDLEY BEAT

Classic Example: "Not Fade Away" (Buddy Holly)

There is a subtle yet distinctive syncopation to this chordal riff that will be best understood by listening closely to Buddy Holly's "Not Fade Away." Other examples can be found in Bo Diddley tracks like "Who Do You Love?" and "Bo Diddley," along with George Michael's acoustic hit from the 80s, "Faith."

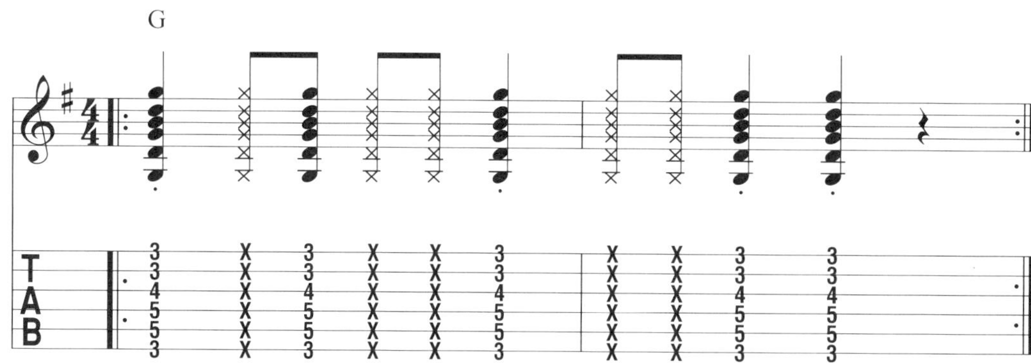

EXAMPLE 21: MAJOR TRIADS

Classic Example: "Can't Get Enough" (Bad Company)

This example uses major triads over a I–IV–V progression, adding the relative IV chord of the C, F, and G chords as decoration. This creates a series of mini I–IV–I progressions: C–F–C, F–B♭–F, and G–C–G. You'll notice that not all these triads are in root position. The F and G triads are in second inversion, (5th on bottom), and the B♭ is in first inversion (3rd on bottom). While C is in root position in the first measure, it's in first inversion in the third measure. It will be helpful to play this one along with a bass player or another instrument laying down the root notes on beat 1 to hear the harmony at work.

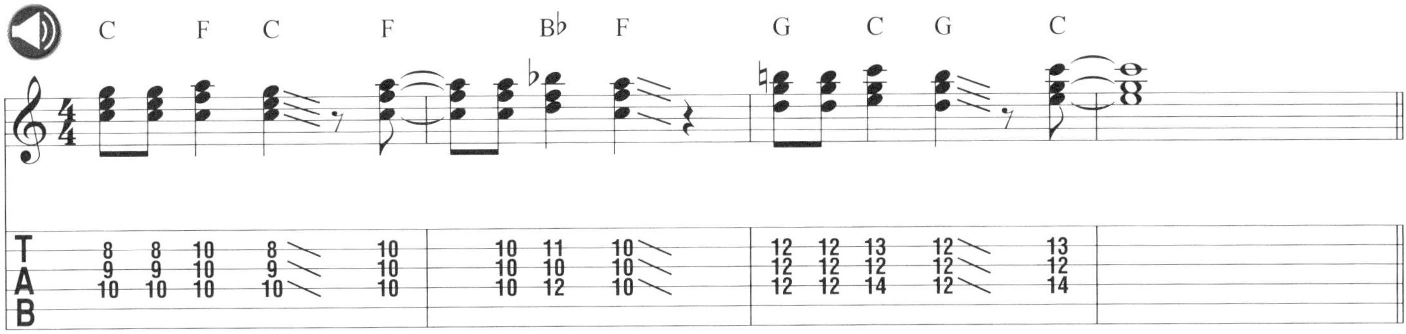

EXAMPLE 22: CHORD MELODY

Classic Example: "Like a Rolling Stone" (Jimi Hendrix)

This example is a short introduction to a rhythmic style utilized by Jimi Hendrix, Keith Richards, and Pete Townshend, among others. The major chords C and F will require a quick position shift on the second beat of each so that the decorative hammer-ons can be accessed with a first-finger barre and a third-finger hammer. For the two minor 7 chords (Dm7 and Em7), hold down the chord while executing the hammer-on and pull-off with the pinky.

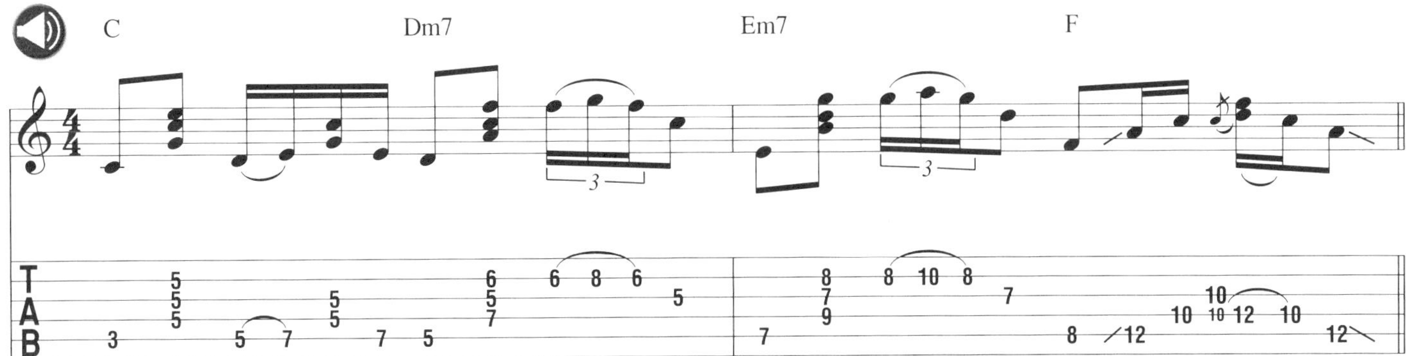

EXAMPLE 23: 50s ROCK 'N' ROLL 1

Classic Example: "Road Runner" (Bo Diddley)

Rhythm guitar in early rock 'n' roll was regularly based on walking bass or cut-boogie bass lines, often with the guitar and bass playing in sync. For both the E and A, use your first finger for second-fret notes, your second finger for third-fret notes, and your third finger for fourth-fret notes. Changing position for the B, use your first finger for the B note, then use the same one-finger-per-fret rule—starting on the fourth fret with your first finger—to play the final riff.

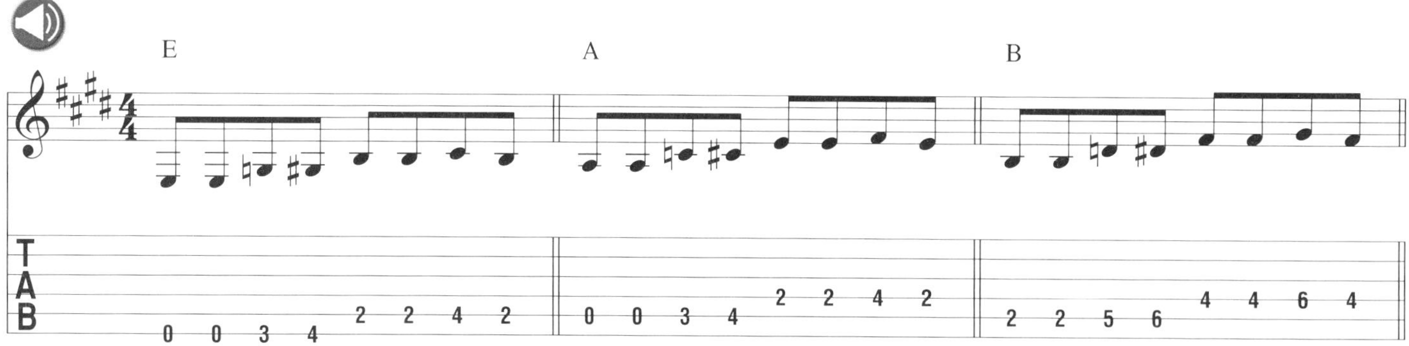

EXAMPLE 24: 50s ROCK 'N' ROLL 2

Classic Example: "Don't Be Cruel" (Otis Blackwell, as performed by Elvis Presley)

Rudimentary though it may be, this riff—consisting of the root, 3rd, and 5th of a major triad—is fundamental to many classics of the era. Simply move the riff to each root note of the I, IV, and V chords, and you're set. As in the previous example, this line is often played in sync with the bass or even a piano. An embellished version can be heard on Elvis Presley's "Don't Be Cruel."

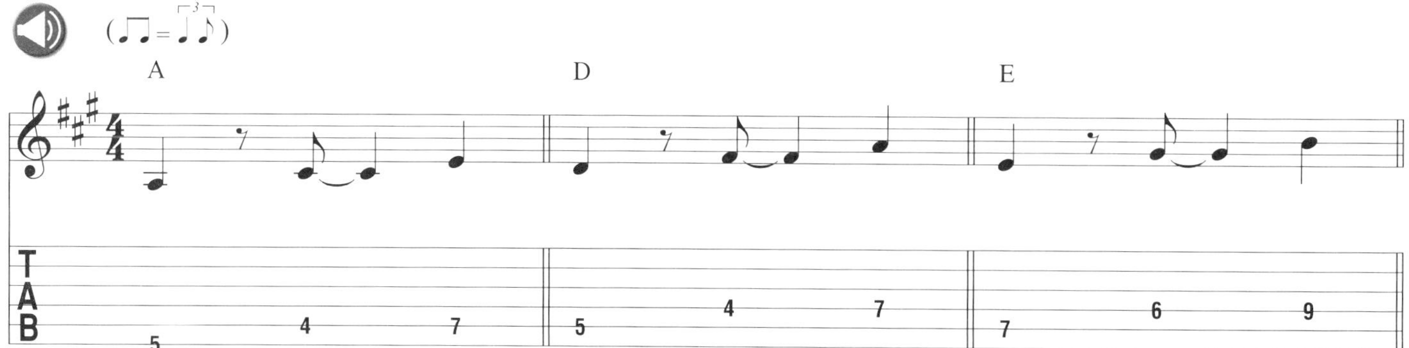

EXAMPLE 25: 50s ROCK 'N' ROLL 3

Classic Example: "Okie Dokie Stomp" (Clarence "Gatemouth" Brown)

Many rock 'n' roll riffs that mimic walking bass lines use the 1, 3, 5, and major 6 of each chord. However, if the progression is made up of dominant 7th chords, an alternative is to substitute the ♭7 in place of the 6. For comparison, listen to "I'm Walkin'" by Fats Domino to hear the major 6 in action and then "Okie Dokie Stomp" by Clarence "Gatemouth" Brown to hear the ♭7.

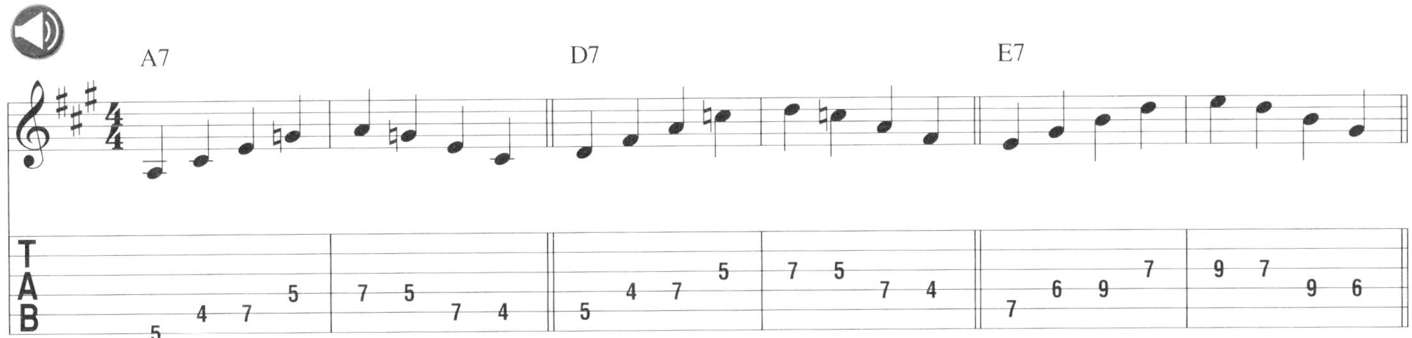

EXAMPLE 26: 50s ROCK 'N' ROLL 4

Classic Example: "Memphis, Tennessee" (Chuck Berry)

One of the more unusual rock 'n' roll patterns, this example is dynamically distinguished by a propulsive, eighth-note hammer-on on beat 4.

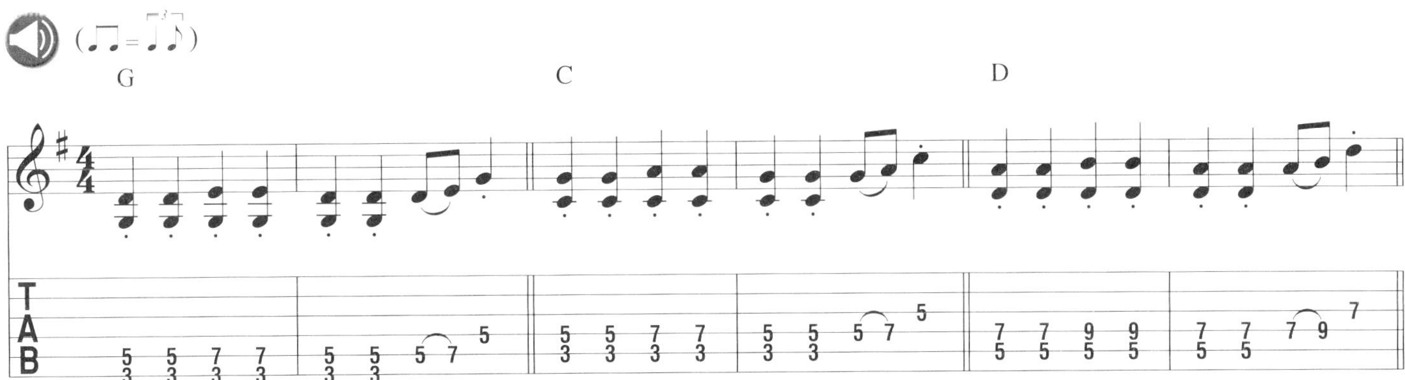

EXAMPLE 27: 60s ROCK

Classic Example: "You Really Got Me" (The Kinks)

A result of bands outgrowing their fascination with American blues, British rockers lead the way in the development of boogie rock—a style that would become the soundtrack of the sixties counter-culture. Funnily enough though, back in the United States, it coincided with the "blues revival." This type of riff has been used numerous times as an unaccompanied intro.

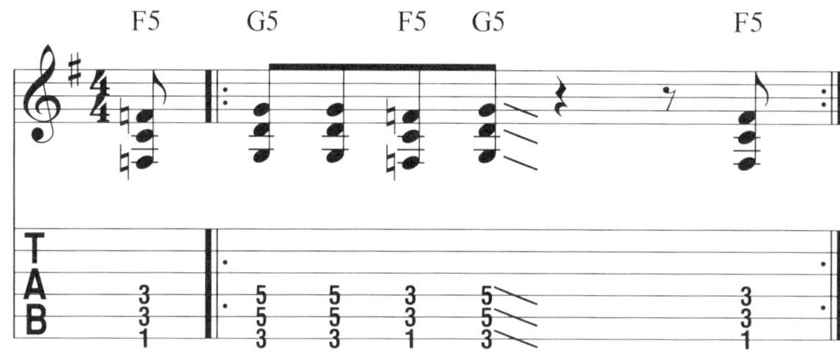

EXAMPLE 28: 60s BOOGIE ROCK

Classic Example: "Mean Town Blues" (Johnny Winter)

Many boogie blues and boogie rock songs are based around the I chord for an entire verse (or even the whole tune). Notated in the key of A, this riff works perfectly in those instances. Examples 28–30 should be played with a shuffle blues feel.

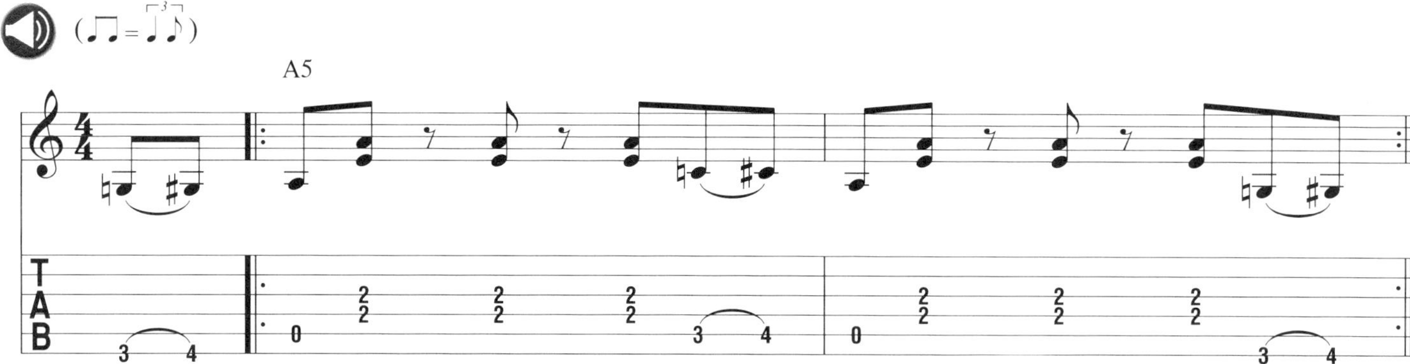

EXAMPLE 29: 70s BOOGIE ROCK 1

Classic Example: "La Grange" (ZZ Top)

In playing this riff, pick direction becomes a crucial element to staying in time. As in Example 14, you'll want to pair downstrokes with downbeats and upstrokes with upbeats. In measure 1, then, we'll play: down-up, up, up, up. Even though we're not playing on the beats 2, 3, and 4, we still move our hand downward ("missing" the strings) to get ready for the next up stroke. For the second measure, our strumming pattern will be: up, up, down, down. While "La Grange" is in the key of A, we've transposed this example to the key of E. Boogie patterns, such as this and the next example, often repeat hypnotically for a number of measures beyond 8, 12, or 16.

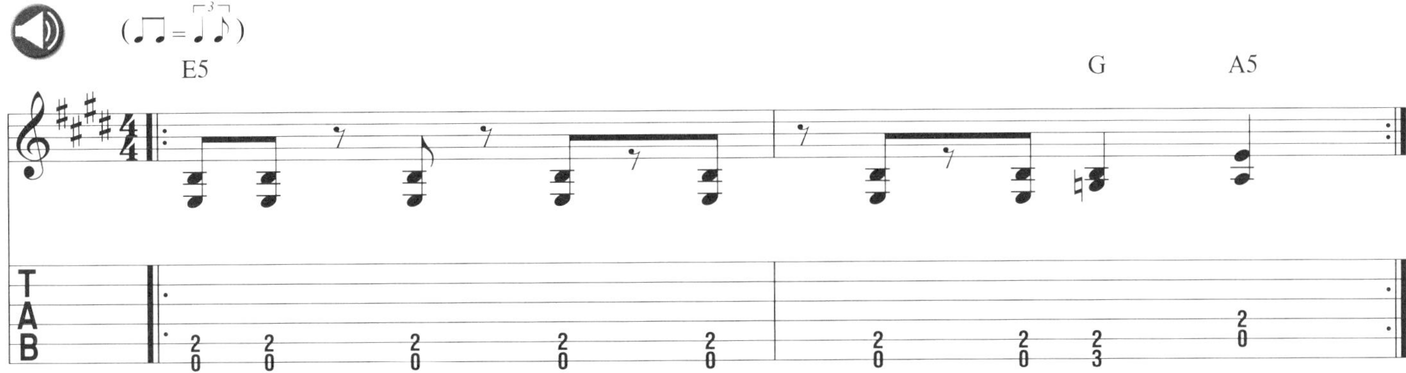

EXAMPLE 30: 70s BOOGIE ROCK 2

Classic Example: "Spirit in the Sky" (Norman Greenbaum)

The same process as Example 29 can be used to ascertain when to use downstrokes and upstrokes in this example as well. Again, using correct pick direction will help greatly with playing in time. We want to pair *down*beats with *down*strokes.

JAZZ

EXAMPLE 31: SWING ERA 1

Classic Example: "Satin Doll"
(Duke Ellington and Billy Strayhorn, with lyrics by Johnny Mercer)

The ii–V–I chord progression has been at the heart of traditional jazz since the "Jazz Age" of the 1920s and 30s. Essentially, the progression provides composers and musicians alike a harmonic device that creates a strong pull back to the I chord. While commonly used to resolve to the tonic, a ii–V can also be placed before any chord to create harmonic movement that enhances simpler progressions. Observe the common tones between Dm7–G7 and Cmaj7–C6.

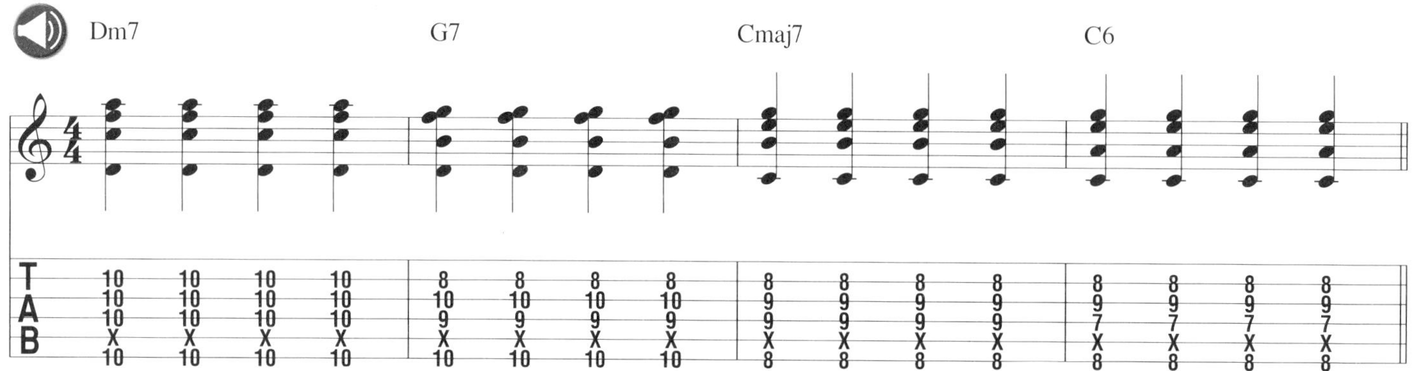

EXAMPLE 32: SWING ERA 2

Classic Example: "Cherokee" (Hank Garland)

Diminished 7th passing chords may sound like the musical equivalent to rocket science, but take heart—they are easy to play and can be a most useful comping tool. In this example, when ascending the harmonized major scale, we connect the I, ii, and iii chords with a diminished 7th chord played on each chromatic passing tone. Check out the chromatic bass line on string 5 from C up to E—a fringe benefit of the four-note chords voiced on the same middle set of strings. The second inversion A7 at the end, while outside the key of C, creates a pull to Dm7, the ii chord.

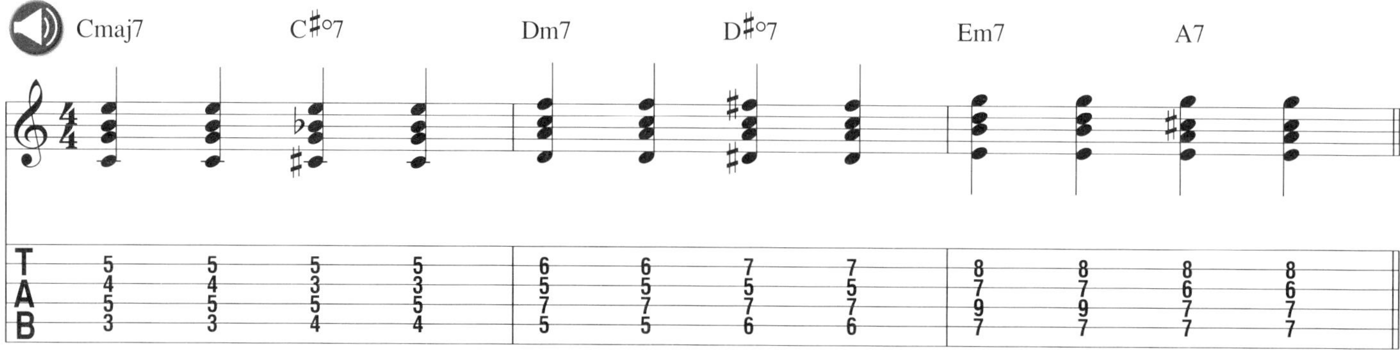

EXAMPLE 33: SWING TO POSTWAR

Classic Example: "Take the 'A' Train"
(Billy Strayhorn, as performed by the Duke Ellington Orchestra)

The most important takeaway from this progression is the slick move from D9 (II) to Dm9 (ii). The musical tension engendered by the major to minor tonality intensifies the resolution to the G13 (V) chord in measure 4. If we consider G13 as the goal, the D9 acts as a secondary dominant—the V chord of G. The resolution of D9 to G is delayed by returning to the diatonic Dm9, which functions as the ii chord within the larger ii–V–I progression in C.

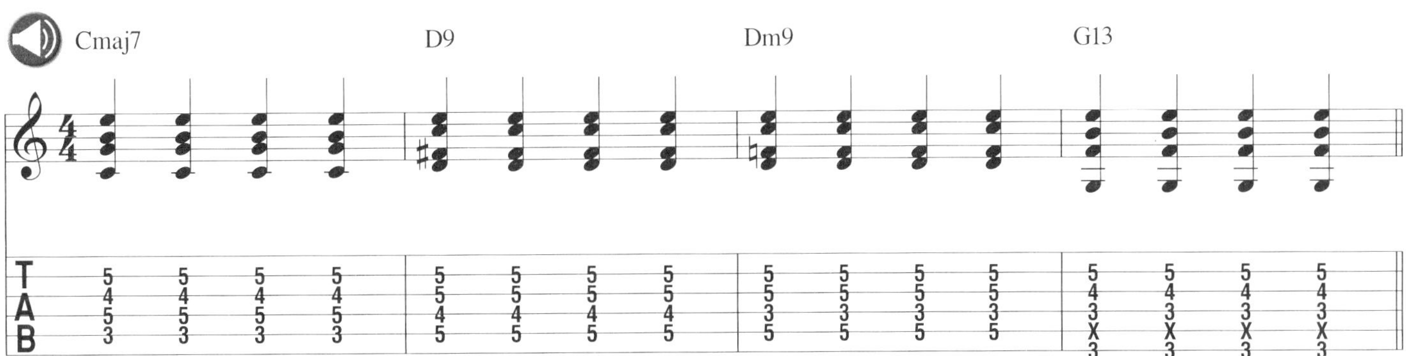

EXAMPLE 34: JAZZ ROCK

Classic Example: "Beyond the Sea"
(Charles Trenet, Jack Lawrence, and Albert Lasry)

This example presents the same ii–V–I pattern as Example 31 but is played using different chord voicings. Both the Dm7 and Cmaj7 are conventional barre chords, while the G7 is played as a voicing referred to as drop 3. Notice the smooth transition between the G7 (V) and Cmaj7 (I). The "secret" is the common tone B and the smooth voice leading of D up to E and F up to G.

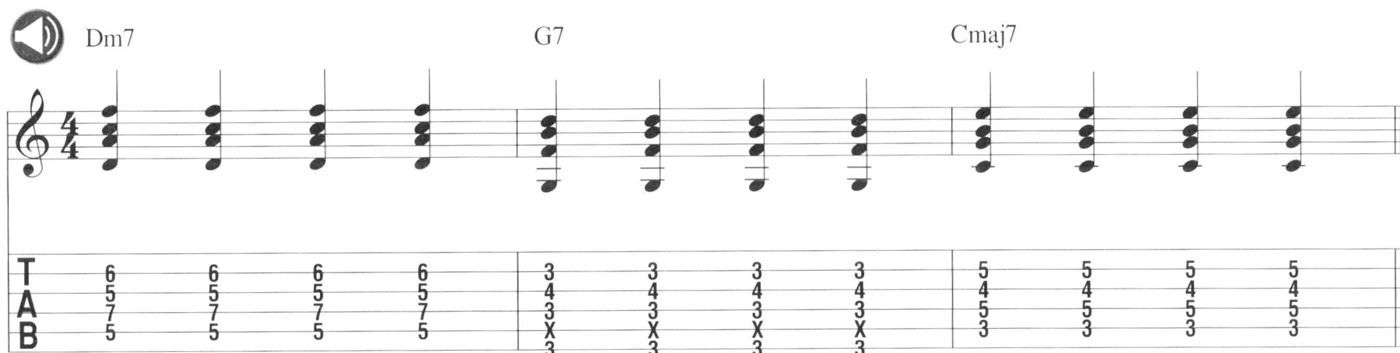

EXAMPLE 35: PREWAR JAZZ 1

Classic Example: "Have You Met Miss Jones" (Richard Rodgers and Lorenz Hart)

The iii–vi–ii–V progression is a commonly used "turnaround"—the last two or four measures of a section. It creates a strong harmonic pull back to the tonic (I) while maintaining smooth voice leading.

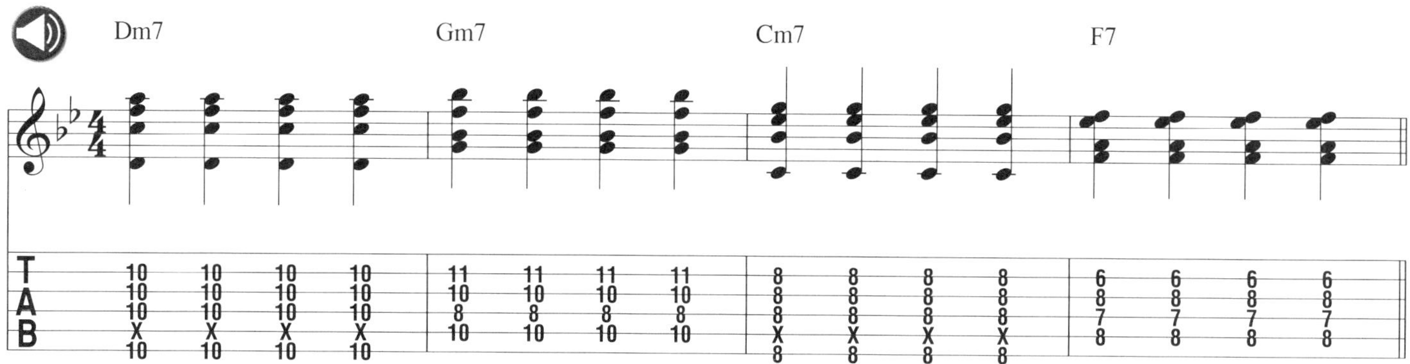

EXAMPLE 36: PREWAR JAZZ 2

Classic Example: I've Got Rhythm (George Gershwin)

When George Gershwin wrote "I Got Rhythm" in 1930, little did he realize that he was creating the template for countless jazz and popular songs that would follow. The two-measure I–vi–ii–V progression lends itself to being recycled, and its use in jazz standards seems endless. For measures 1 and 3, and again in measure 7 and 8, the I chord is substituted by the iii chord, and the vi chord is changed to a dominant 7. This creates a stronger ii–V pull to Dm7 and delays the V–I cadence until the end of the four-measure form.

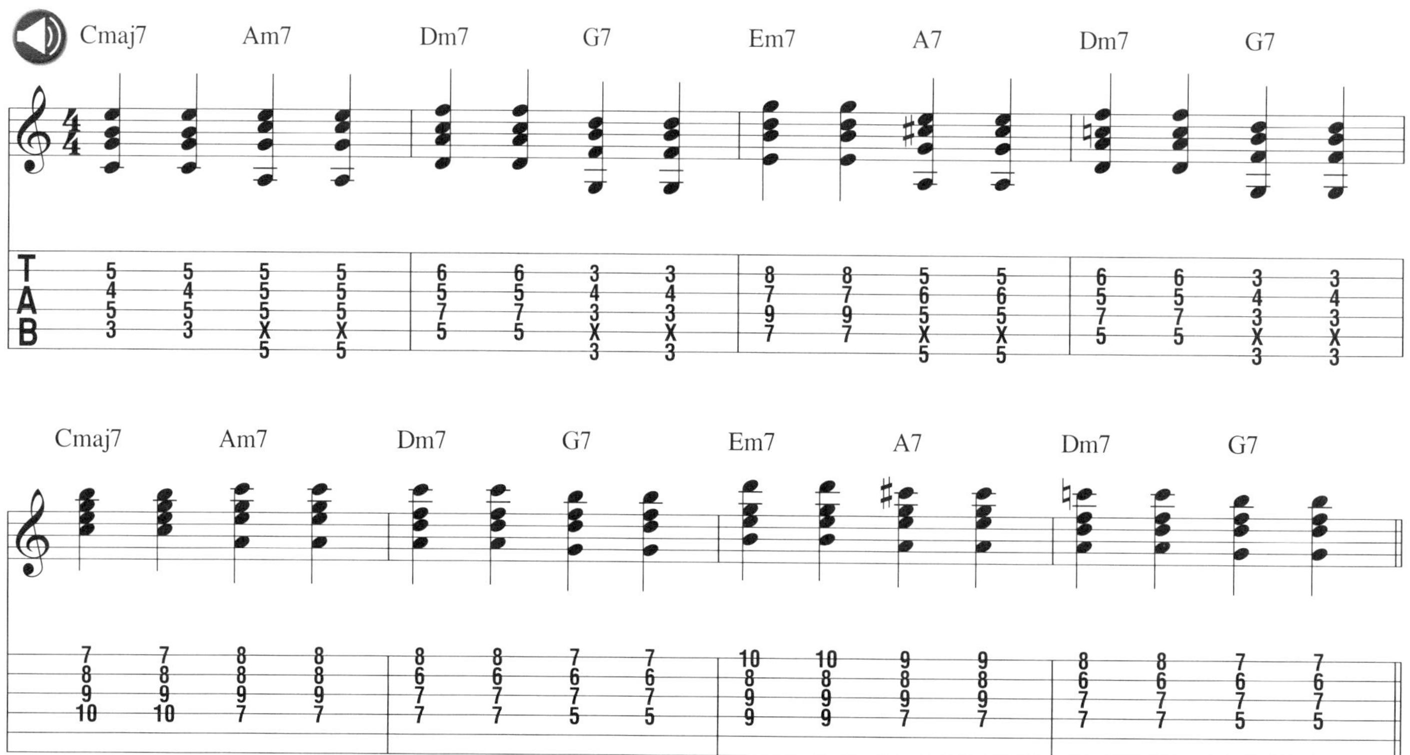

EXAMPLE 37: PREWAR JAZZ AND BEYOND

Classic Example: "My Funny Valentine" (Richard Rogers and Lorenz Hart, as performed by Miles Davis)

This example is immediately recognizable and, along with many jazz standards, it can be heard in numerous pop and rock songs, such as "Michelle," "Stairway to Heaven," and "Into the Great Wide Open." Start with a minor barre chord for Cm (extend the barre through strings 1-4 in preparation for the coming moves), then replace the root (C) on the fourth string, 10th fret, with B (major 7th) on the ninth fret, using your second finger. Next, lift the second finger to sound the Cm7 with a first-finger barre. Finally, for Cm6, use your first finger on the fourth string and barre strings 3-1 with your third finger.

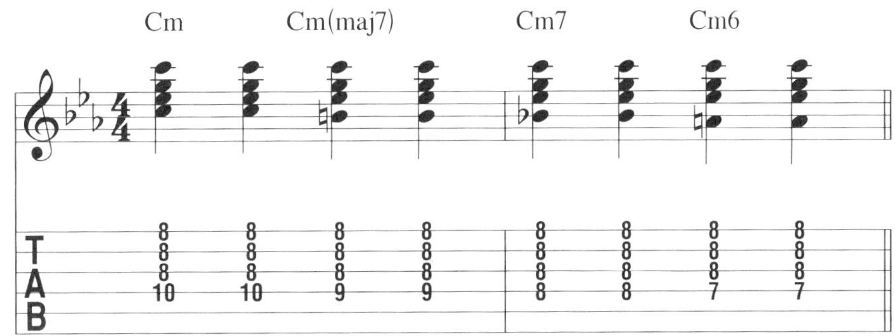

EXAMPLE 38: JAZZ ARPEGGIOS 1

Classic Example: "Shivers" (Lionel Hampton and Charlie Christian)

Arguably the improvisational foundation of jazz guitar, if not all jazz instruments, *arpeggios* are crucial to single-note playing over jazz progressions. While entire instructional books have been written on the topic, we'll start here by simply outlining the chord tones of a ii–V–I progression in C. This riff can be transposed to any key by moving it up or down the fretboard. The Charlie Christian guitar solo in "Shivers" is a perfect example of a solo using arpeggios.

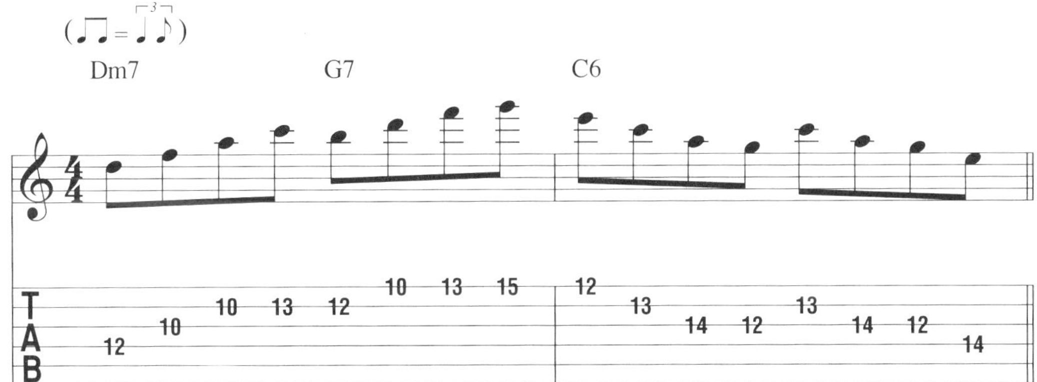

EXAMPLE 39: JAZZ ARPEGGIOS 2

Classic Example: "Rose Room" (Art Hickman and Harry Williams, as performed by the Benny Goodman Sextet with Charlie Christian on guitar)

This example is taken from the Charlie Christian solo in "Rose Room." Christian uses several arpeggio fragments to outline the I7–IV opening. The hook emphasizes the ♭7 (G♭) and the major 3rd (C) while adding the 9th (B♭) as a variation over the I7 chord. Christian finishes with a descending Cmin7♭5 arpeggio that, over an A♭7, provides the 3rd, 9th, 7th, and 5th chord tones. Over the D♭maj7, the line starts with a chromatic passing tone (D) to the root D♭, before ascending up D♭maj7. On the descending run, a B♭m7 arpeggio is used over the D♭maj7, giving the sound of a D♭6 chord.

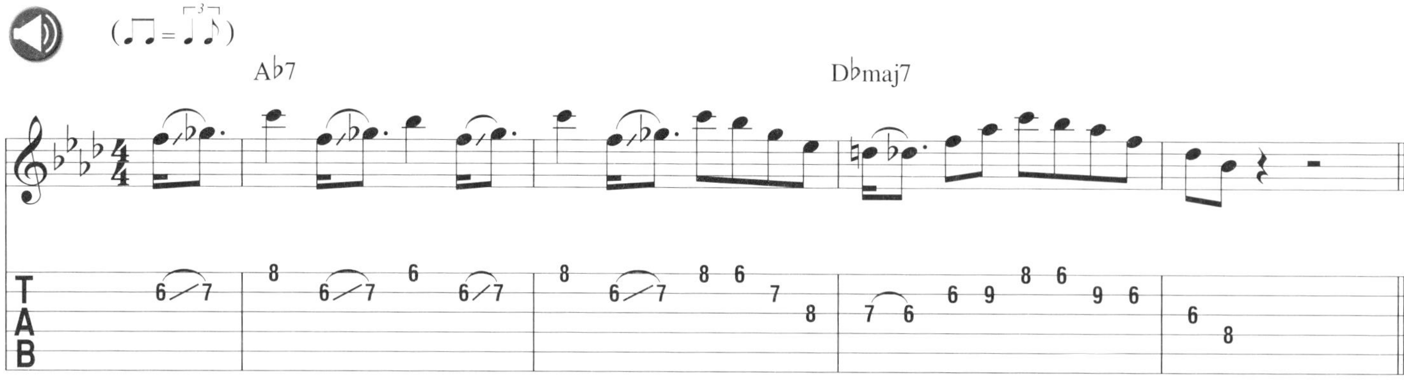

EXAMPLE 40: JAZZ ARPEGGIOS 3

Classic Example: "Grand Slam" (Benny Goodman Sextet with Charlie Christian on guitar)

This example is a solo fragment over the I chord (F7) of a jazz blues progression. Arpeggios are utilized over the F7 to add extensions and dissonance. You could analyze this as a D minor arpeggio with an additional chromatic run up the first string. Over an F7 chord, it implies an F13 sound with the repeated use of the D note. This motif can be heard in Charlie Christian's solo from "Grand Slam."

COUNTRY

EXAMPLE 41: BLUEGRASS 1

Classic Example: "Gallopin' Guitar" (Chet Atkins)

I-IV and I-V changes appear in country music almost as frequently as they do in the blues. Bluegrass, a precursor to country music featuring the banjo, mandolin, fiddle, and guitar, often involved arpeggios and other picking techniques. This example utilizes a B♭ triad for the first measure and then the upper structure of an F7 chord in the second measure, creating a repeating rhythmic figure that outlines the harmony. Regarding the picking, though Chet would use a thumbpick and two fingers to roll through these arpeggios, a hybrid picking approach (pick for string 4, middle finger for string 3, and ring finger for string 2) works equally well.

EXAMPLE 42: BLUEGRASS 2

Classic Example: "Foggy Mountain Breakdown" (Lester Flatt and Earl Scruggs)

Perhaps the most recognizable bluegrass lick of all time, the G-run has been used time and time again. These two examples by Lester Flatt—one ascending and one descending—epitomize the bluegrass guitar sound and will be a welcome addition to your arsenal of riffs. Both use the G major pentatonic scale with the chromatic B♭ leading to the major 3rd (B) each time.

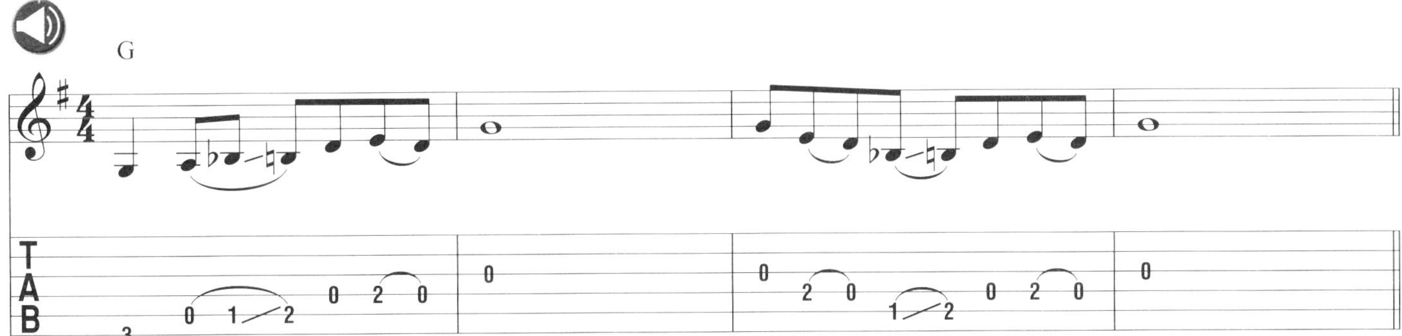

EXAMPLE 43: POSTWAR NASHVILLE 1

Classic Example: "Hey, Good Lookin'" (Hank Williams)

First-position chords—often referred to as open chords or "cowboy chords"—were synonymous with country music up until the late 1940s when electric guitars began to hold sway. However, to this day, first-position chords are considered the backbone of country music. Hold the partial C chord and move only your third finger to alternate the bass notes C and G. Play the F chord with your thumb over the top of the fretboard or as a full E-shape barre chord on the first fret. The D7 is easier because the alternating bass notes are simply the open fourth and fifth strings. The full G7 can be held throughout the fourth measure as you alternate the bass notes between the sixth and fifth string.

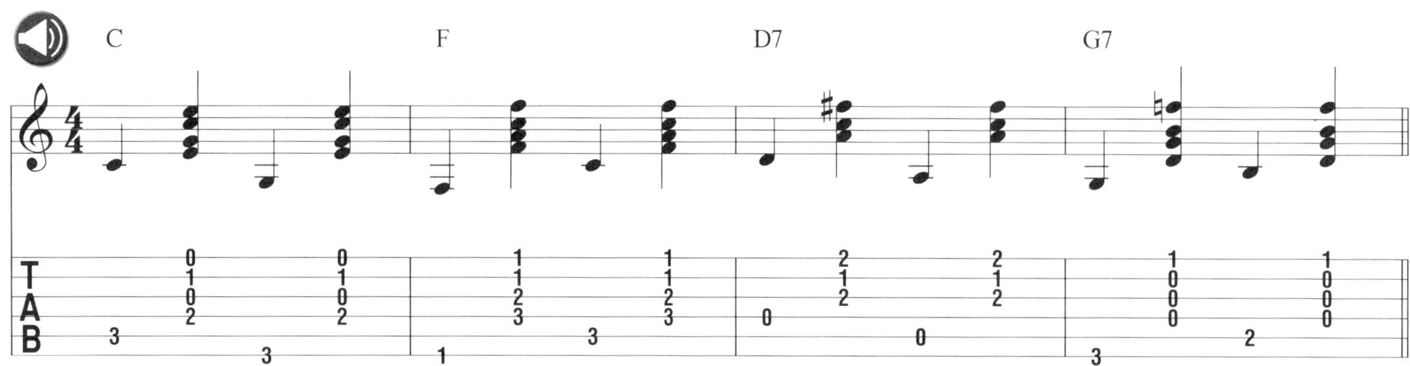

EXAMPLE 44: POSTWAR NASHVILLE 2

Classic Example: "Country Gentleman" (Chet Atkins and Boudleaux Bryant)

Example 44 presents an accessible I–IV progression in the key of A. Because it is fully fretted, the shapes can be moved to any key. In the first measure, barre the top three strings at the ninth fret, then use your fourth finger on the 12th fret of the fifth string, your third finger on the 11th fret of the fourth string, and your second finger on the 10th fret of the second string. To play the second measure, move the partial barre up to the 10th fret, then form an E shape with your second, third, and fourth fingers.

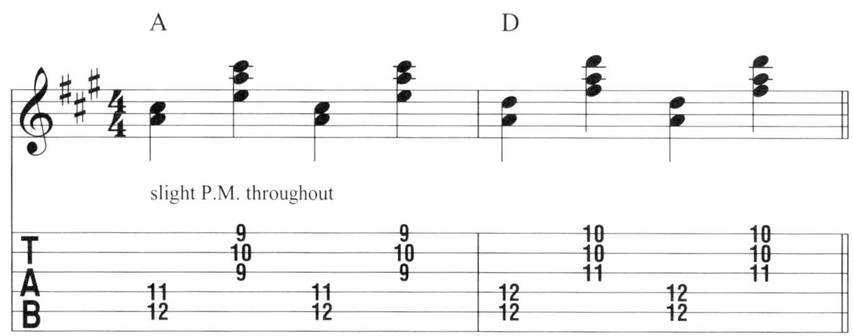

EXAMPLE 45: POSTWAR NASHVILLE 3

Classic Example: "I'm So Lonesome I Could Cry" (Hank Williams)

This is a great riff to use over a I–V–I turnaround. In the pick-up measure, a diatonic step-wise line starting on the 5th (B) leads right to the root E on the downbeat of the second measure. Next, the chromatic move from G to G♯ is used to first move to the V chord (B7) and then back to the I chord (E). This dissonance and resolution will be familiar to your ears as a country staple.

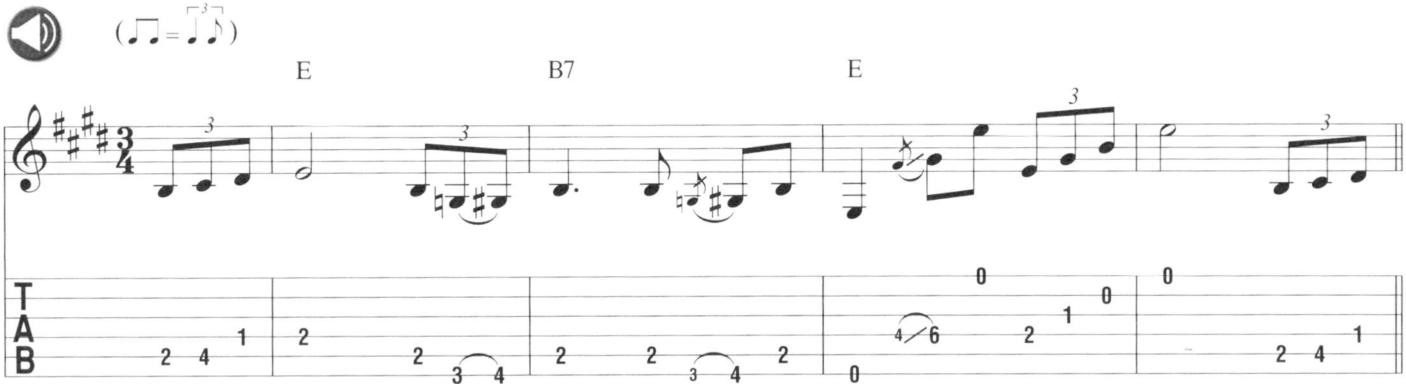

EXAMPLE 46: COUNTRY ROCK 1

Classic Example: "Amie" (Pure Prairie League)

Broken chord licks are found in both country and country-rock music. Quite simply, they "dress up" common chord changes while also contributing to the forward motion. Efficient fingering is paramount to creating the rolling rhythm that characterizes this riff. For each chord, use a partial barre on strings 4-2. To execute the hammer-on for the A and G chords, start with the first-finger barre and the second finger placed on the second string, then use your third finger for the hammer-on. For the slide on the fourth beat of the D chord, keep the partial barre in place but only pluck the third string.

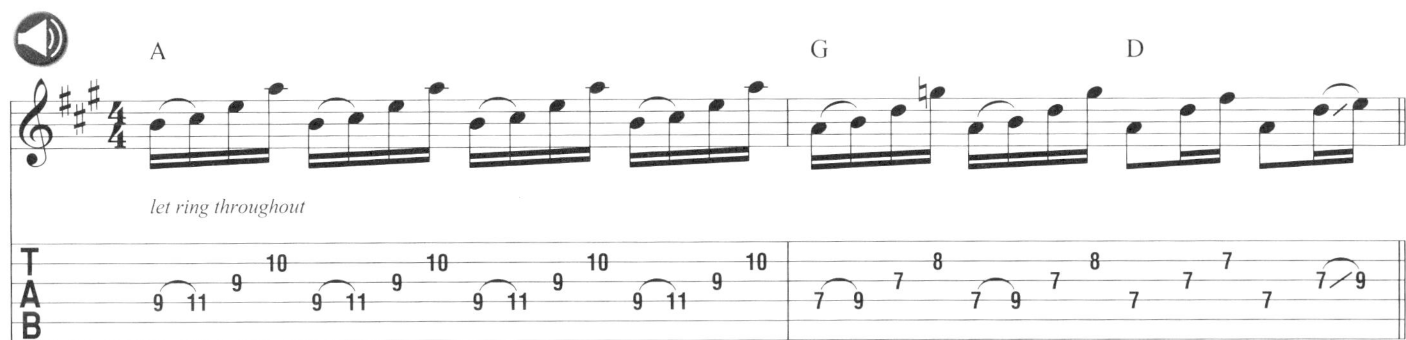

EXAMPLE 47: COUNTRY ROCK 2

Classic Example: "Buckaroo" (Buck Owens)

In the 1950s, a raucous brand of proto-country-rock developed in Bakersfield, California. Known as "honky tonk," it was epitomized by Buck Owens and his lead guitarist, Don Rich. In the first measure, play a "cowboy" D chord and arpeggiate up to the open first string before hammering on to the second fret (F♯). Instead of using a partial barre, you will have to fret the A chord in the second measure with individual fingers. This enables you to play the open and fretted notes of the figure along the second string. This example simplifies the "Buckaroo" form to a three-measure I–V–I–IV–V. Use hybrid picking in measure 2, with the pick for the open fifth string and the middle and ring fingers for the dyads.

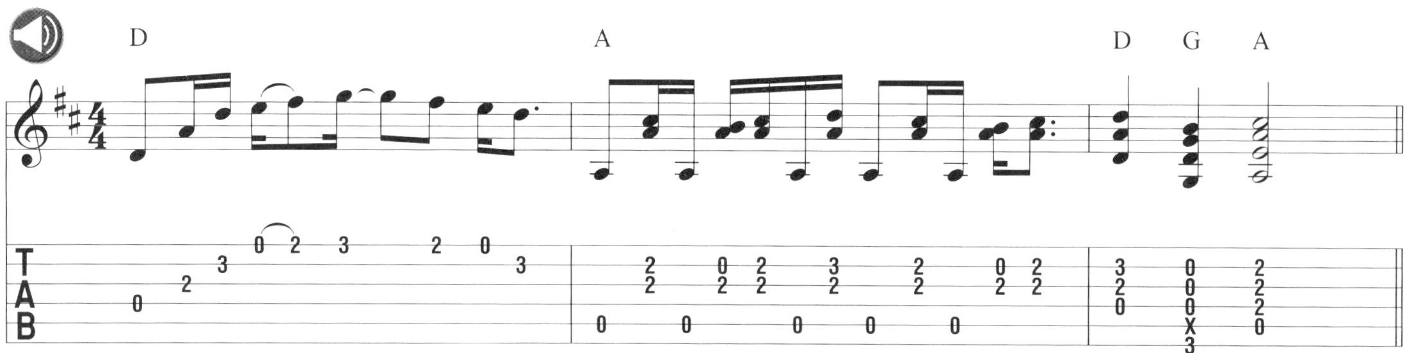

EXAMPLE 48: COUNTRY ROCK 3

Classic Example: "Little Sister" (Doc Pomus and Mort Shuman, as performed by Elvis Presley)

As it does with virtually all American vernacular music, the blues also permeates country music. Here, the E blues scale in used as the signature riff in Elvis's recording of "Little Sister." Bend the G note on the first string a 1/4 step with the third finger, then on beat 4, use your second and third fingers to manage the hammer-on and pull-off sequence on the third string. (Alternatively, start with your second finger for the bend and use your first and second fingers for the hammer-on and pull-off.)

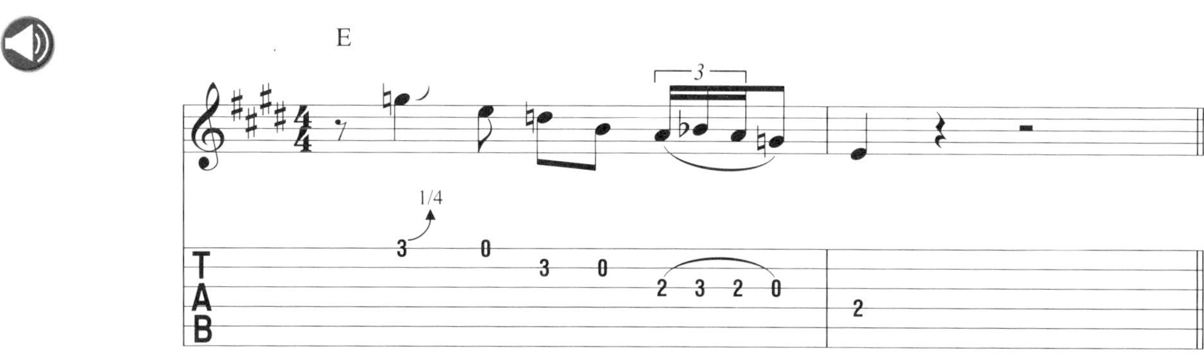

EXAMPLE 49: MODERN NASHVILLE 1

Classic Example: "Heartbroke" (Guy Clark)

Over time, country music in Nashville and other Southern locales expanded on first-position chord vocabulary and started to include triads played on the strings 3-1. Another compositional advancement was the expansion of harmonic material to include more than just the I, IV, and V chords. This example stems from the instrumental break found in "Heartbroke" by Guy Clark, where the ii, iii, and vi chords—Em, F♯m, and Bm, respectively—are used alongside the IV and V, providing a welcome break from the I-IV-V form of the verses. Note that all the triads in this example are in second inversion, with the 5th on bottom. (Note: The original "Heartbroke" is in the key of B, whereas this example has been presented in the key of D.)

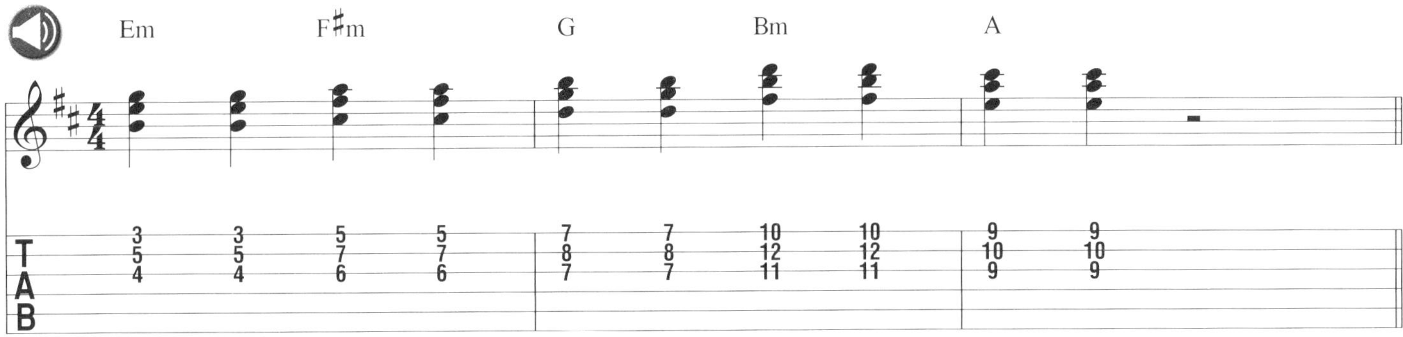

EXAMPLE 50: MODERN NASHVILLE 2

Classic Example: "The Only Daddy That Will Walk the Line" (Jimmy Bryant, as performed by Waylon Jennings)

This riff sounds great over a dominant 7th chord, highlighting the root, 5th, and 7th chord tones, while adding color with the major 6th, ♯9th, and 9th. It stems from the composite blues scale: a combination of both the major and minor blues scales. You end up with a nine-note scale: 1-2-♭3-3-4-♭5-5-6-♭7. Combining the two opens the door to more melodic possibilities and the ability to create tension and release.

GUITAR NOTATION LEGEND

Guitar music can be notated three different ways: on a *musical staff*, in *tablature*, and in *rhythm slashes*.

RHYTHM SLASHES are written above the staff. Strum chords in the rhythm indicated. Use the chord diagrams found at the top of the first page of the transcription for the appropriate chord voicings. Round noteheads indicate single notes.

THE MUSICAL STAFF shows pitches and rhythms and is divided by bar lines into measures. Pitches are named after the first seven letters of the alphabet.

TABLATURE graphically represents the guitar fingerboard. Each horizontal line represents a string, and each number represents a fret.

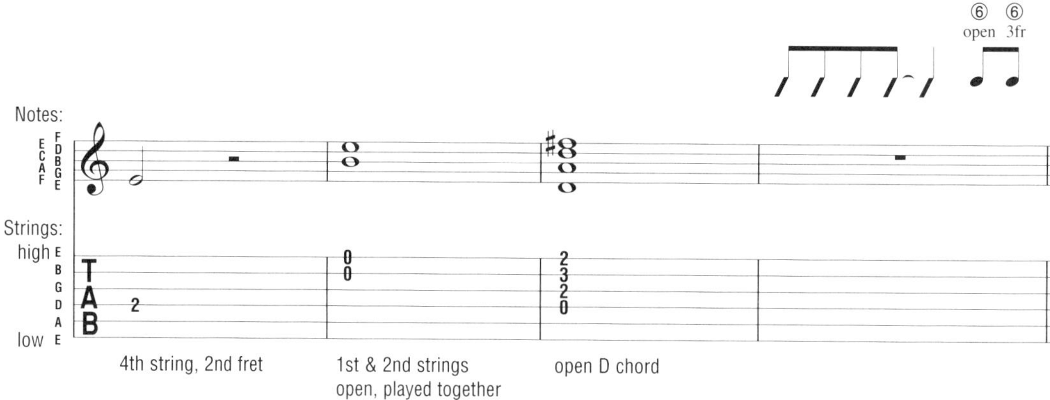

Definitions for Special Guitar Notation

HALF-STEP BEND: Strike the note and bend up 1/2 step.

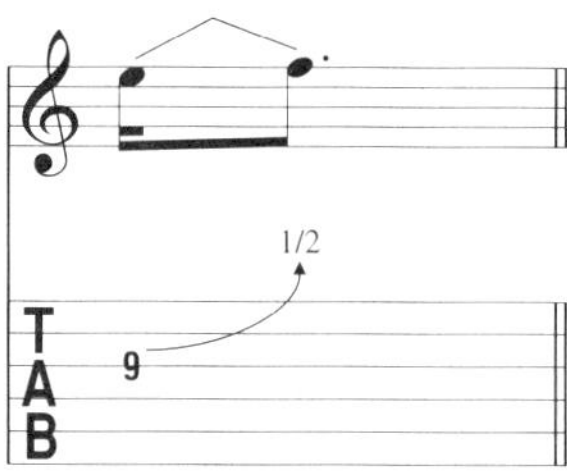

WHOLE-STEP BEND: Strike the note and bend up one step.

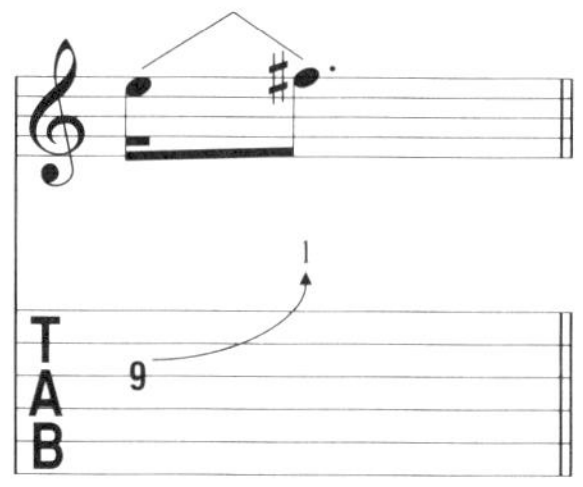

GRACE NOTE BEND: Strike the note and immediately bend up as indicated.

SLIGHT (MICROTONE) BEND: Strike the note and bend up 1/4 step.

BEND AND RELEASE: Strike the note and bend up as indicated, then release back to the original note. Only the first note is struck.

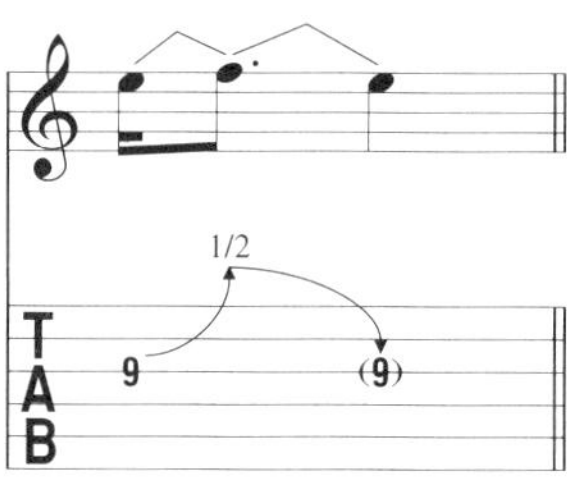

PRE-BEND: Bend the note as indicated, then strike it.

PRE-BEND AND RELEASE: Bend the note as indicated. Strike it and release the bend back to the original note.

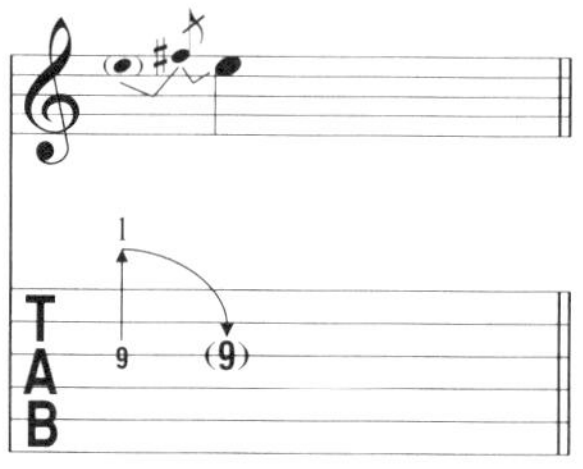

UNISON BEND: Strike the two notes simultaneously and bend the lower note up to the pitch of the higher.

VIBRATO: The string is vibrated by rapidly bending and releasing the note with the fretting hand.

WIDE VIBRATO: The pitch is varied to a greater degree by vibrating with the fretting hand.

HAMMER-ON: Strike the first (lower) note with one finger, then sound the higher note (on the same string) with another finger by fretting it without picking.

PULL-OFF: Place both fingers on the notes to be sounded. Strike the first note and without picking, pull the finger off to sound the second (lower) note.

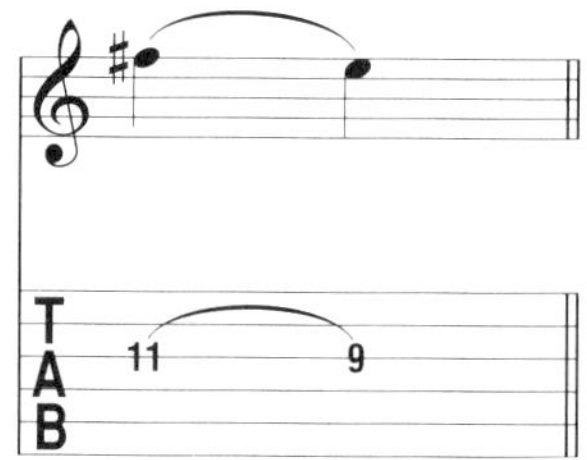

LEGATO SLIDE: Strike the first note and then slide the same fret-hand finger up or down to the second note. The second note is not struck.

SHIFT SLIDE: Same as legato slide, except the second note is struck.

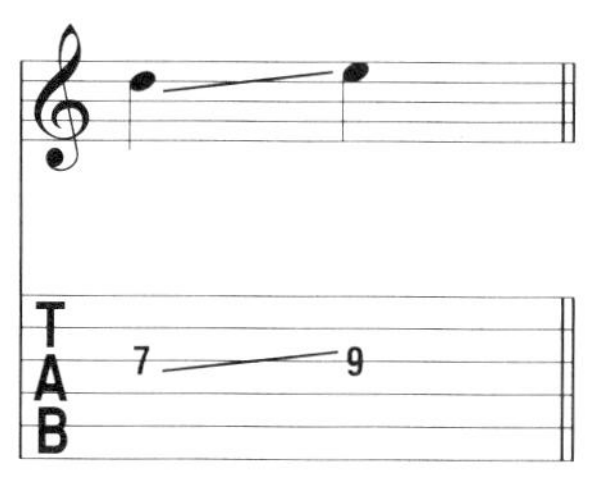

TRILL: Very rapidly alternate between the notes indicated by continuously hammering on and pulling off.

TAPPING: Hammer ("tap") the fret indicated with the pick-hand index or middle finger and pull off to the note fretted by the fret hand.

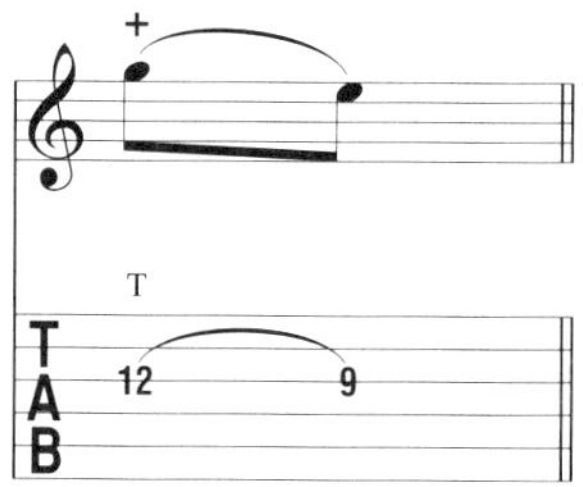

NATURAL HARMONIC: Strike the note while the fret-hand lightly touches the string directly over the fret indicated.

PINCH HARMONIC: The note is fretted normally and a harmonic is produced by adding the edge of the thumb or the tip of the index finger of the pick hand to the normal pick attack.

HARP HARMONIC: The note is fretted normally and a harmonic is produced by gently resting the pick hand's index finger directly above the indicated fret (in parentheses) while the pick hand's thumb or pick assists by plucking the appropriate string.

PICK SCRAPE: The edge of the pick is rubbed down (or up) the string, producing a scratchy sound.

MUFFLED STRINGS: A percussive sound is produced by laying the fret hand across the string(s) without depressing, and striking them with the pick hand.

PALM MUTING: The note is partially muted by the pick hand lightly touching the string(s) just before the bridge.

RAKE: Drag the pick across the strings indicated with a single motion.

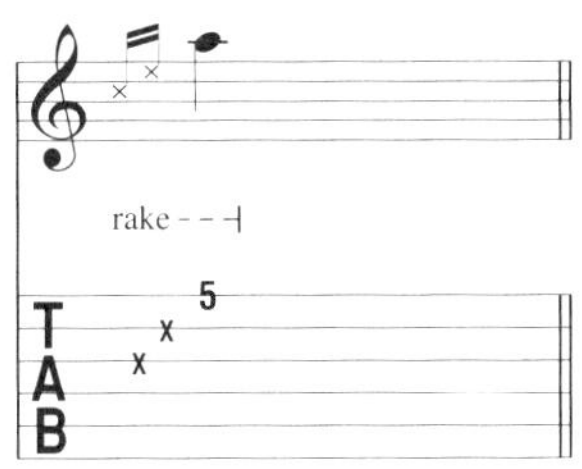

TREMOLO PICKING: The note is picked as rapidly and continuously as possible.

ARPEGGIATE: Play the notes of the chord indicated by quickly rolling them from bottom to top.

VIBRATO BAR DIVE AND RETURN: The pitch of the note or chord is dropped a specified number of steps (in rhythm), then returned to the original pitch.

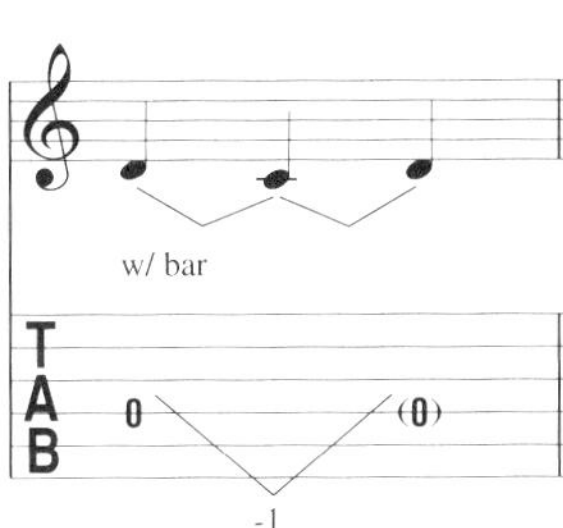

VIBRATO BAR SCOOP: Depress the bar just before striking the note, then quickly release the bar.

VIBRATO BAR DIP: Strike the note and then immediately drop a specified number of steps, then release back to the original pitch.

Additional Musical Definitions

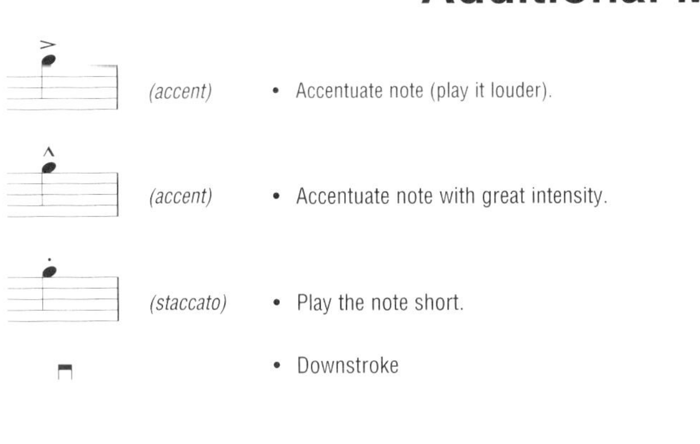

(accent) • Accentuate note (play it louder).

(accent) • Accentuate note with great intensity.

(staccato) • Play the note short.

• Downstroke

V • Upstroke

D.S. al Coda • Go back to the sign (𝄋), then play until the measure marked "*To Coda*," then skip to the section labelled "**Coda**."

D.C. al Fine • Go back to the beginning of the song and play until the measure marked "*Fine*" (end).

Rhy. Fig. • Label used to recall a recurring accompaniment pattern (usually chordal).

Riff • Label used to recall composed, melodic lines (usually single notes) which recur.

Fill • Label used to identify a brief melodic figure which is to be inserted into the arrangement.

Rhy. Fill • A chordal version of a Fill.

tacet • Instrument is silent (drops out).

• Repeat measures between signs.

1. 2. • When a repeated section has different endings, play the first ending only the first time and the second ending only the second time.

NOTE: Tablature numbers in parentheses mean:

1. The note is being sustained over a system (note in standard notation is tied), or
2. The note is sustained, but a new articulation (such as a hammer-on, pull-off, slide or vibrato) begins, or
3. The note is a barely audible "ghost" note (note in standard notation is also in parentheses).

FIRST 50

Books in the First 50 series contain easy to intermediate arrangements for must-know songs. Each arrangement is simple and streamlined, yet still captures the essence of the tune.

First 50 Baroque Pieces You Should Play on Guitar
Includes selections by Johann Sebastian Bach, Robert de Visée, Ernst Gottlieb Baron, Santiago de Murcia, Antonio Vivaldi, Sylvius Leopold Weiss, and more.
00322567

First 50 Bluegrass Solos You Should Play on Guitar
I Am a Man of Constant Sorrow • Long Journey Home • Molly and Tenbrooks • Old Joe Clark • Rocky Top • Salty Dog Blues • and more.
00298574

First 50 Blues Songs You Should Play on Guitar
All Your Love (I Miss Loving) • Bad to the Bone • Born Under a Bad Sign • Dust My Broom • Hoodoo Man Blues • Little Red Rooster • Love Struck Baby • Pride and Joy • Smoking Gun • Still Got the Blues • The Thrill Is Gone • You Shook Me • and more.
00235790

First 50 Blues Turnarounds You Should Play on Guitar
You'll learn cool turnarounds in the styles of these jazz legends: John Lee Hooker, Robert Johnson, Joe Pass, Jimmy Rogers, Hubert Sumlin, Stevie Ray Vaughan, T-Bone Walker, Muddy Waters, and more.
00277469

First 50 Chords You Should Play on Guitar
American Pie • Back in Black • Brown Eyed Girl • Landslide • Let It Be • Riptide • Summer of '69 • Take Me Home, Country Roads • Won't Get Fooled Again • You've Got a Friend • and more.
00300255

First 50 Classical Pieces You Should Play on Guitar
Includes compositions by J.S. Bach, Augustin Barrios, Matteo Carcassi, Domenico Scarlatti, Fernando Sor, Francisco Tárrega, Robert de Visée, Antonio Vivaldi and many more.
00155414

First 50 Folk Songs You Should Play on Guitar
Amazing Grace • Down by the Riverside • Home on the Range • I've Been Working on the Railroad • Kumbaya • Man of Constant Sorrow • Oh! Susanna • This Little Light of Mine • When the Saints Go Marching In • The Yellow Rose of Texas • and more.
00235868

First 50 Guitar Duets You Should Play
Chopsticks • Clocks • Eleanor Rigby • Game of Thrones Theme • Hallelujah • Linus and Lucy (from *A Charlie Brown Christmas*) • Memory (from *Cats*) • Over the Rainbow (from *The Wizard of Oz*) • Star Wars (Main Theme) • What a Wonderful World • You Raise Me Up • and more.
00319706

First 50 Jazz Standards You Should Play on Guitar
All the Things You Are • Body and Soul • Don't Get Around Much Anymore • Fly Me to the Moon (In Other Words) • The Girl from Ipanema (Garota De Ipanema) • I Got Rhythm • Laura • Misty • Night and Day • Satin Summertime • When I Fall in Love • and more.
00198594

First 50 Kids' Songs You Should Play on Guitar
Do-Re-Mi • Hakuna Matata • Let It Go • My Favorite Things • Puff the Magic Dragon • Take Me Out to the Ball Game • Won't You Be My Neighbor? (It's a Beautiful Day in the Neighborhood) • and more.
0030050099

First 50 Licks You Should Play on Guitar
Licks presented include the styles of legendary guitarists like Eric Clapton, Buddy Guy, Jimi Hendrix, B.B. King, Randy Rhoads, Carlos Santana, Stevie Ray Vaughan and many more.
00278875 Book/Online Audio

First 50 Riffs You Should Play on Guitar
All Right Now • Back in Black • Barracuda • Carry on Wayward Son • Crazy Train • La Grange • Layla • Seven Nation Army • Smoke on the Water • Sunday Bloody Sunday • Sunshine of Your Love • Sweet Home Alabama • Working Man • and more.
00277366

First 50 Rock Songs You Should Play on Electric Guitar
All Along the Watchtower • Beat It • Brown Eyed Girl • Cocaine • Detroit Rock City • Hallelujah • (I Can't Get No) Satisfaction • Oh, Pretty Woman • Pride and Joy • Seven Nation Army • Should I Stay or Should I Go • Smells like Teen Spirit • Smoke on the Water • When I Come Around • You Really Got Me • and more.
00131159

First 50 Songs by the Beatles You Should Play on Guitar
All You Need Is Love • Blackbird • Come Together • Eleanor Rigby • Hey Jude • I Want to Hold Your Hand • Let It Be • Ob-La-Di, Ob-La-Da • She Loves You • Twist and Shout • Yellow Submarine • Yesterday • and more.
00295323

First 50 Songs You Should Fingerpick on Guitar
Annie's Song • Blackbird • The Boxer • Classical Gas • Dust in the Wind • Fire and Rain • Greensleeves • Road Trippin' • Shape of My Heart • Tears in Heaven • Time in a Bottle • Vincent (Starry Starry Night) • and more.
00149269

First 50 Songs You Should Play on 12-String Guitar
California Dreamin' • Closer to the Heart • Free Fallin' • Give a Little Bit • Hotel California • Leaving on a Jet Plane • Life by the Drop • Over the Hills and Far Away • Solsbury Hill • Space Oddity • Wish You Were Here • You Wear It Well • and more.
002875599

First 50 Songs You Should Play on Acoustic Guitar
Against the Wind • Boulevard of Broken Dreams • Champagne Supernova • Every Rose Has Its Thorn • Fast Car • Free Fallin' • Layla • Let Her Go • Mean • One • Ring of Fire • Signs • Stairway to Heaven • Trouble • Wagon Wheel • Yellow • Yesterday • and more.
00131209

First 50 Songs You Should Play on Bass
Blister in the Sun • I Got You (I Feel Good) • Livin' on a Prayer • Low Rider • Money • Monkey Wrench • My Generation • Roxanne • Should I Stay or Should I Go • Uptown Funk • What's Going On • With or Without You • Yellow • and more.
00149189

First 50 Songs You Should Play on Solo Guitar
Africa • All of Me • Blue Skies • California Dreamin' • Change the World • Crazy • Dream a Little Dream of Me • Every Breath You Take • Hallelujah • Wonderful Tonight • Yesterday • You Raise Me Up • Your Song • and more.
00288843

First 50 Songs You Should Strum on Guitar
American Pie • Blowin' in the Wind • Daughter • Hey, Soul Sister • Home • I Will Wait • Losing My Religion • Mrs. Robinson • No Woman No Cry • Peaceful Easy Feeling • Rocky Mountain High • Sweet Caroline • Teardrops on My Guitar • Wonderful Tonight • and more.
00148996

HAL•LEONARD®
www.halleonard.com

1223
014